New Track, New Life

Kimberly Godwin Clark

Printed in the United States of America
First Printing, 2008
Revised and Updated 2024
ISBN: 978-0-9985048-2-7

ACKNOWLEDGMENTS

I would like to express my gratitude to Aaron Comenetz for lending his advice, time, editing, and photography skills to this book.

Cover photo of Two Punch Willy by Frank Padula.

Back cover photo of author with Sand Save by Katherine Turnbull Photography.

PROLOGUE

Kimberly Godwin Clark always had a passion for Thoroughbreds. That passion has produced many retired racers that have gone on to successful second careers, including the 4* eventer Houdini (registered name, Rocky Times) and Breeder's Bridge to High Performance Winner Constant Star.

For 30 years Clark galloped, trained and owned Thoroughbred racehorses. She learned to gallop under the tutelage of the great steeplechase rider John Bosley and then went on to the racetrack with Ann Merryman, a second-generation horseman. She spent most of her professional riding career at Old Hilltop, Pimlico Racecourse, in Baltimore, Maryland, but also rode in Florida for several winters before settling at Leighton Farm in 2007 to begin her new venture in retraining retiring racehorses for new careers.

Her training program is based on knowledge she has gained from a lifetime of working with racehorses and now the incredible guidance she receives from each horse that comes through the Leighton Farm program. She introduces each horse to the fundamentals of relaxation, balance, straightness and rhythm to create a solid foundation for any discipline.

Since Clark began promoting off the track Thoroughbreds for sale or adoption in 2007, the response has been phenomenal. On her own and through her nonprofit, Thoroughbred Placement Resources, she has rehomed over 1,000 retired racehorses. But many more need homes.

Clark believes that anyone with a working knowledge of horses and the desire to learn can succeed with an ex-racehorse, if they are properly informed. She wrote this book to explain how racehorses are trained, how they think, and how they live at the track. By providing this information, Clark hopes to correct many of the misconceptions about Thoroughbreds. They are not inherently crazy or dangerous; in fact, most are intelligent, kind, generous and eager to please if they are properly transitioned into new careers. They come in all shapes, sizes, temperaments and levels of athletic ability. You will not find a better equine partner.

PREFACE

I created this book to help every retired Thoroughbred racehorse find success in their new lives. Thoroughbred Placement Resources needs your help to continue our work. Without supporters like you, this cannot happen.

We are always looking for new volunteers to help with every aspect of our work. Fundraising plays a huge role in how many horses we can assist each year. Please consider holding a fundraiser to support our work and to help us continue to help retiring racehorses find new lives when their careers end. Please make it possible for us to offer support to those who take these fine horses into their lives.

You can help by donating, volunteering and spreading the word.

Go to https://www.goodhorse.org/or call 410-802-8425 to find out how you can help.

My Sincere Thanks,

Kimberly Godwin Clark

Monetary donations can be mailed to TPR, 13130 Molly Berry Road, Upper Marlboro, MD 20772

CONTENTS

1 WHY CHOOSE A THOROUGHBRED OFF THE TRACK?

If you wish to pursue a riding discipline that requires athleticism, generosity and intelligence, then the Thoroughbred ex-racer is an excellent choice. Thoroughbreds are smart and sensitive animals. They are extremely generous. I admit I am biased because this is my breed of choice. They have so much to offer it was easy to be swayed their way. Thoroughbred racehorses are fantastic athletes because they are bred to be just that.

Retired racehorses come with a solid foundation for their next job. They are well-developed both physically and mentally for performance from their beginning. Their bodies and minds have been conditioned for work. They are ridden almost every day resulting in a solid work ethic. I know of no other way to purchase a horse that has had access to daily medical care, consistent training and handling by professionals.

Retired racers have been trained and ridden by professionals from the start. There are very few amateurs within the racing industry. Racehorses are handled consistently from the age of one year. By the age of two, they are worldly compared to most other breeds. They have had exposure to all sorts of vehicles, tractors, water trucks, and every color and size of horse – except for maybe minis. They are usually good shippers because regular travel is a part of racing.

Racehorses are already prepared to work around other horses. They train both with and around other horses while doing completely different activities. They have learned how to focus on their job while 25 or more horses are training around them. Activities of the other horses include galloping, jogging, breezing, breaking from the gate and even acting up. This is good preparation for transitioning to the warmup ring at a horse show, riding in groups on trails, or being in the field during a fox chase.

Racehorses receive daily handling including grooming, bathing, therapy and training. Few other horses are exposed to so many different people on a regular basis. It is normal for them to have lots of different riders throughout their career. Even if there is a regular daily rider, the jockey on race day is usually different. Grooms come and go at the track. There are vets, blacksmiths, the owner, trainer, exercise riders, just to name a few of the people who are important in the racehorse's daily life.

Imagine the cost in time and money to expose and educate a horse to all of this, and how uneventful a horse show or any other event really is to most retired racers.

How racehorses are started

Young racing prospects must get their start by learning to be ridden. They will likely begin their careers at a large training facility or a small private farm. Traditionally, yearlings are green broke in the fall and given most of the winter months off to grow and develop. They return to training in the early spring as two-year-olds. Today, with milder winters, all weather footing and the desire to make horse training more economical, many continue training throughout the winter so they can get to the track in the early spring. Some owners and trainers wait to start their horses until early in their two-year-old year, especially if the horse is big or the breeding is known to produce late bloomers.

Riding babies is an amazing experience. These equine children learn quickly. The people who work with babies are a special breed. Not all exercise riders are comfortable riding babies. Patience and the ability to "sit chilly" meaning stay cool, keep focused and to banish all fear, under some very exciting circumstances, are mandatory. Oftentimes riders who work with babies on the farm follow them to the track. This practice provides continuity between rider and horse, providing confidence for the youngster in the new experience of racetrack life.

For East Coast racing, most of the large training facilities are in the south. The Carolinas and Florida offer weather that allows consistent training throughout the year. Large facilities can have well over a hundred horses in training. Training tracks are available at most of the larger farms. This allows the youngster to be familiar with their future workspace from the start, but also limits the education that will be helpful to his future after racing. OTTB trainers need to be mindful of this. As is true in every equestrian discipline, each facility has its own program to teach the young horse how to become a racehorse. The most popular way today is to start them in a stall or round pen and go right to the training track. There are advantages and disadvantages to starting a horse this way. The focus in this type of training is track readiness – period.

Racehorses are not taught how to be ridden as beasts of burden; they are only prepped on the skills necessary for racing. Many racehorses in America have more muscle development on their left side due to running counterclockwise and doing their most intense work in this direction. They do train in both directions though, which is worth mentioning. Hills and uneven ground are rare encounters for lots of horses that begin their careers in facilities such as these. This style of starting horses does not cater to the show/pleasure world. However, with good retraining that provides a solid foundation, these horses can do almost anything after retirement from racing.

Smaller facilities usually do not have a training track. Babies receive individual attention creating an atmosphere where the youngster is allowed to be a horse some of the time rather than 100% of the focus being on becoming a racehorse. There is often more time to spend with these soon to be racehorses. Many trail ride and are ridden quietly with others hacking out. When available, hills are used to build wind. They must learn to balance themselves when they gallop across uneven ground in the fields. I have done my fair share of starting racehorses on my small farm over the years. The advantages in getting a horse started this way are numerous if you're looking for a show/pleasure horse.

It's worth mentioning here that the job of the racehorse is to win races, not carry the rider the way show and pleasure horses are trained to do. The job of the exercise rider or jockey is to stay out of the racehorse's way. So, you will have a lot of explaining to do when you begin to retrain your retired racer, no matter how he was started.

I don't believe where a horse began his career is a reason to buy or not buy a particular horse, but there is no such thing as too much information. If you can find out how he was started it will help you plan a more thorough re-education.

photo by Katherine Turnbull Photography

Where do trainers and owners get horses?

Understanding how owners and trainers select and acquire their racing prospects will demonstrate the differences and similarities between the pleasure/show and racing ways of shopping for a horse. For the most part, trainers and owners purchase horses without the pre-purchase exam (PPE) that is common in other disciplines. There is a "buy them and try them" mentality for many involved in racing. This is one reason some trainers and owners lose their patience with people from other disciplines where it is common to have a vet check. Most of the time they are not hiding anything. They have trouble understanding why you cannot go over the horse yourself to see if he is suitable for your purposes, especially if the horse is being given away or sold for a small amount of money. It is quite normal to buy a horse off of his racing form, sight unseen. Many trainers do not ride, so not riding the horse before purchase is also normal to them.

Purchase at auction is another popular way to get a racehorse or prospect. Prospective buyers are not allowed to ride the horses before purchase. There are several basic types of auctions. Most common are weanling and yearling auctions. Weanlings are commonly turned out to grow after being purchased and when the horse is a yearling he begins the training process. These auctions are usually held in the fall when the yearlings at the sale are ready to begin work. They are usually vetted before the sale and it is quite expensive to gain access to their x-rays and other diagnostic records. The two-year-olds in training sales are a very popular way to buy a prospect. These sales last several days to a week when the potential buyers can watch horses train and breeze short distances. The actual auction is held at the end of this period. Horses are vetted during these sales. Most of the time radiographs are available in a repository to be viewed by buyers and vets for a healthy fee.

Claiming races are another common way to get a racehorse. An advantage is that the horse is already racing. The trainer or owner places the correct amount of money in his account at the racetrack and then drops a claim slip some 15 minutes before post time of the race. When the starting gate doors open, he is the owner of the horse unless more than one slip is dropped. In that case the new owner is decided by lottery. The horse is not vetted by the would-be purchaser. Most of the time the prospective trainer and/or owner watch him in the paddock before making the claim. Sometimes they may watch the horse for several preceding races before deciding to claim. The decision to purchase a horse in this manner is primarily made on his racing form/history. When a claimed horse is not sound after a race, the claim is voided.

A trainer or owner may hear about a horse that's for sale through the grapevine, or he may get a call from a trainer whom he has bought from in the past. Unless there is a lot of money at stake, this horse would be purchased sight unseen and off his race record and the other trainer's word.

There is a hierarchy to racing. Individual tracks have their own level of competitive difficulty. A trainer at a tougher track will have little trouble selling his non-performers to trainers located at tracks where the competition is less. Usually, these trainers do not vet and they will show up the same day they are contacted, with cash to pick up the horse. There are times when owners or trainers buy a prospect privately with a PPE. The price is often the determining factor in deciding if a PPE is done.

Why trainers and owners retire a horse

Lack of talent or desire to race is probably the most common reason. Believe it or not, most Thoroughbreds never win even one race and these horses make some of the best show prospects. A horse may have talent but lack the competitive nature necessary to be a racehorse. Slow at the track is still very fast for most people outside racing. Most any retired racer will likely be fast enough for your purposes.

Each trainer has a limited number of stalls assigned at the track. He is expected to make a certain number of starts per stall each month. A trainer or owner may elect to sell the untalented horse, and bring one in that hopefully has more promise.

If the horse has an injury that requires time off – even with a great prognosis to return to racing – his owner may decide to get rid of him rather than doing the rest and rehab. It takes quite a bit of time to get the horse back to racing fitness after the time off. Unless the horse is a great racehorse, it often just isn't worth the investment.

Horses can become ineligible to race for a variety of reasons, including if they are deemed unsound by a track veterinarian. Such horses are placed on the "Veterinarian's List," also known as the vet's list. The Horseracing Integrity and Safety Authority (HISA), which enforces a "national, uniform set of integrity and safety rules" applicable to "every Thoroughbred racing participant and racetrack facility" has detailed rules governing when a horse must be placed on the Vet's list and when he can again become eligible to race. Another powerful list is the Starter's List in the Secretary's office. This is for horses that refused to break from the gate. A horse can be permanently barred from racing for this.

Each racing jurisdiction has a set of rules and qualifications for the horses to be allowed to race under their governance. There is a cut off age for maidens. Maidens are horses who have never won a race. In most jurisdictions, if a horse has not won a race by a certain age, he is ineligible to race. If a horse has run for a claiming price that is less than the bottom claiming price in a particular jurisdiction, he cannot be entered or stabled in that jurisdiction. At the writing of this book, in Maryland, the bottom is $5,000, so if the horse is run in a $2,500 claiming race in another state, he can no longer race in Maryland until he later finishes 1, 2, or 3 for $5,000. There are other ways to become ineligible, but these are the most common.

What happens to racehorses when they retire from racing?

Magnificent Mr. Z

Race trainers are in the business of training racehorses so when a horse is no longer competitive or capable of racing, they must get them off the track. Racing is not a job as much as a way of life for everyone on the backstretch, including trainers. There is not much time for socializing outside of the racing world. When a trainer wants to sell a horse, he knows lots of other trainers to call. So, the easiest way for most trainers to move a horse on is to sell him or her to a trainer at a lesser track. Most trainers can pick up the phone and have another trainer at a less competitive track buy the horse almost immediately. No vetting and a cash sale. Many times the horse is gone in less than 24 hours.

Another option is to send the horse to auction. Some trainers have horses picked up by a person who takes them to auction. This is done on demand or on a certain day of the week. Any auction, no matter how fancy, has kill buyers lurking in the outskirts waiting to see if someone just wants to get rid of a horse. There are weekly auctions held throughout the country. These are not the kind of auctions where racing prospects are sold. The majority of horses at these auctions are bought by "meat men" who ship them to plants in Mexico and Canada. They are killed in horrible ways and then slaughtered for their meat. This is something that should never happen to any horse, and if we want racing to survive, it must stop happening to Thoroughbreds. Racing needs the public to embrace and love racing. The public is not likely to fall in love with racing if the star, the equine athlete will be tortured, killed and eaten when he fails to be competitive. This is my opinion and one of the reasons I am trying to help retired racehorse owners retrain their horses for new careers. I know that the bigger the market for sport Thoroughbreds, the fewer ex-racehorses will be sent to slaughter.

Nowadays most tracks have zero tolerance slaughter policies. For example, the following is Maryland's policy: "The Stronach Group has formally adopted a company-wide policy promoting the humane treatment of racehorses, announced on October 10, 2009. Under the policy, any trainer or owner stabling at a Maryland Jockey Club [MJC] facility who directly or indirectly participates in the transport of a horse from an MJC facility to either a slaughterhouse or an auction house engaged in selling horses for slaughter will be prohibited from having stalls at any MJC facility. The policy also applies to any actions related to the transport of a horse from an MJC facility where the ultimate intended result is a horse's slaughter." Tracks and the racing industry are also funding retirement organizations and even creating "in house" aftercare programs. There are some very successful examples throughout the country. Unfortunately, racehorses are still being slaughtered.

My favorite way for a Thoroughbred to retire from racing is transitioning to a new career. This is the best option for everyone involved. When I say career, it could be companion, eventer, jumper, dressage horse, broodmare, trail horse, faithful sidekick—you name it. Thoroughbreds are smart, generous and athletic; they can do anything given good guidance and a chance. I am far from the only professional that recognizes the ability and talent of the Thoroughbred.

There are lots of rescue groups who can assist trainers and owners in finding a good home for a horse who has retired from racing. I hate that word rescue, because most racehorses do not need to be rescued, they just need an opportunity. A better word for these organizations is Aftercare. They specialize in transitioning horses from racing to other careers. Some give horses evaluation rides while others put real training on the horse before they are offered for adoption. Some actually do rescue horses who have ended up in the kill pens at auctions. Still others help horses who've been injured while racing heal and find a new path in life once they are ready. Many organizations do a combination of these things. Thoroughbred Placement Resources, Inc., my organization is one of these charities.

2 LIFE AT THE RACETRACK

Knowledge of your new horse's past life will help make the transition from racehorse to riding horse much smoother for your horse. To begin with, there is a very predictable, regular routine at most tracks. This is due in part to the training hours of most tracks and training centers. Most tracks open for training at 5:30 or 6 a.m. They usually close all training facilities around 10 to 11 a.m. Southern tracks may open and close earlier to beat the heat. Horses thrive when they live in a predictable environment. They are more confident when they can count on scheduled events such as feeding, training, and rest times. Race day is the day where there is deviation. On that day most trainers walk the horse early in the morning. There are those horses that go to the track early but they usually train very lightly. All other care and duties are scheduled around the time of the race.

A typical day at the track varies little from stable to stable. It begins around 4 a.m. with the grooms arriving. Some outfits feed a small meal first. Water buckets and feed tubs are cleaned. The stalls are mucked and bandages removed for leg inspection. Horses that are not training that day are walked by hand. Those who are to be ridden are groomed, saddled and sent to the track where they might jog, gallop or breeze. Upon the horse's return to the barn, the groom and hot walker are waiting to take the horse from the rider, who is eager to get on their next mount.

If it's warm enough, the horse gets a bath before he is hand walked or after he trains. If it's cool, they place a cooler on him.

Either way the horse is walked for 20 to 30 minutes. After the day's training, it is time for grooming, therapy and rest. The farrier may be scheduled; a massage, chiropractic adjustments, acupuncture or other therapy treatments are done as needed. As the morning activities wind down the horse is fed his breakfast and left to relax for the remainder of the day. His dinner is typically between 4 to 5 p.m. Some horses are fed a small meal upon the groom's arrival in the morning, too.

Horses at the track are handled very differently from the way show and riding horses are handled. Much must be explained to the horse once he is no longer in a race training environment. Below is an overview of some of the more obvious things that are done differently at the track.

- All four of the racehorse's feet are picked from the left side of the horse.
- Horses are tied on a tie chain located in the back of their stall and never out in the open as in the shed row of the barn or on cross ties.
- They move over with the voice command "over", while being worked on or when the stall is being cleaned.
- Horses are walked around the shed row in a counterclockwise direction. They are allowed to pull against the person walking them, jig, kick out, or otherwise play.
- Racehorses are also allowed to jig and play while being ridden to and from the track. The rider disregards this behavior and just sits there very relaxed. The horse is expected to stop this behavior and focus on training when it's time to gallop or work. Racehorses are allowed to be strong and do a fair amount of carrying on at times. However, they are expected to go directly from this behavior to receptive when necessary.
- Fit racehorses are trained to do as asked during their "highest" times; for example, on race day upon entering the paddock, the horse identifier checks the horse as he enters the paddock. At that moment, most racehorses are excited and "on the muscle" because they are anticipating racing. But each horse stops and stands for the identifier. The lesson is: do not think your new horse won't listen to

you when he's reacting strongly to something. Chances are when you tell him to behave, he will.

- Most racehorses are good shippers. When there is a problem getting a retired racehorse on a trailer, people who are unfamiliar with racehorses tend to assume that the horse thinks he is going to the races and doesn't want to go. That couldn't be further from the truth. Most horses I have known love to race. Usually, the reason why they won't load is far simpler. The people may be unsure of themselves, which is alarming to the horse because it never happens in the racing world, or the trailer being used is not the type the horse is accustomed to. For instance, most racehorses have never been on a "tag along"or bumper pull trailer. They've never walked into something that looks so cramped. They need a moment to realize you really do want them to go into that tiny area. Most racehorses are accustomed to shipping on horse vans or roomy trailers. But patience will prevail. If you work with the horse and apply a bit of patience with firm encouragement, they will eventually go on a tag along and learn to be comfortable.

What racehorses eat

The quality and quantity of food the average racehorse receives is stunning to most people unfamiliar with the rigors of racing. The average horse at the track receives about 14 pounds of high quality 11% or 12% protein sweet feed every day. Some horses are fed even more. The physical demands of racing require maximum effort from the horse. On top of these demands, most racehorses are young and still growing. It is not uncommon for a Thoroughbred to continue growing through the age of five; some do not finish until they are seven years old. Remember this when you are assessing prospects at the track.

High quality timothy hay along with alfalfa is fed free choice.

Often hay nets filled to the maximum are found hanging outside the door of each stall. The horse can look out his stall door and munch hay all day. This practice helps with the nervous tendencies that can be created by a bored horse. Some trainers feed a bran mash once a week or after a race. It is easy on the digestive system of the hard-working racehorse, and much appreciated after the stress of exertion during a race. Supplements, electrolytes, multivitamins, joint supplements, vitamin E and selenium, blood builders, ulcer treatments, just to name a few of the things that may be added to the athlete's diet. Horsemen at the track ask so much of their horses, they feel a responsibility to give them all nutritional support possible. This diet, fed consistently, would make the calmest horse high in spirits.

The people who work with racehorses

All persons who work on the backstretch of licensed racetracks must be licensed by the state in which they work. This includes trainers, hot walkers, grooms and jockeys. Vendors, vets, blacksmiths and even owners must be licensed to enter the backstretch. All licensees undergo a criminal background check complete with fingerprinting. They are subject to random drug tests as well. Trainers must have worked on the backstretch for a minimum of two years before they are eligible to take the trainer's test. Exercise riders undergo a trial period in which they must demonstrate competent riding skills. This license can be taken away at any time if the rider is deemed dangerous or incompetent.

Grooms

Grooms are the fundamental caretakers of the racehorse. Normally this is a salaried position. Oftentimes a groom is responsible for the care of four horses. Their duties include all direct care of the horses they are assigned. These duties include tacking up, getting the rider on, and taking the horse from the rider when he comes back from the track. The groom administers any therapy or additional care such as bandaging legs, ultrasound, nebulizer, magnetic therapy, ice, etc.

Race day brings its own set of responsibilities for the groom, including all morning preparations and pre-race protocols. Grooms accompany the horse on the van or trailer to the racecourse. The van departs at a specified time and being late is not an option. The groom stays with the horse in the receiving barn until the race. He is responsible for getting the horse ready to run. The horse has to be bridled, may need bandages applied, and the groom is responsible for any other preps before he takes the horse over to the paddock.

Grooms lead the horse to the paddock at a specified time and then hold the horse while the trainer saddles him. The horse is then led to the track once the jockey is mounted. Most horses are handed off to pony riders, who escort horse and jockey to the starting gate. The groom picks the horse up on the track after the race and holds him while the jockey and his valet unsaddle him. He then leads the horse back to the receiving barn to cool him out. This is a very long day for the groom. The day may begin at 4:00 a.m. and not end until the wee hours of the next morning if the horse is in a late race. The groom is there in the barn the next morning to care for their charges on time.

Being a groom is a very demanding job, both physically and mentally. Most grooms are devoted to their horses and work long hours to give them a competitive edge and a good life. Trust me when I tell you they are not doing this for the money, most do it for the love of the horse.

Hotwalkers

A hot walker does just that, he or she walks the horse until he has cooled down after training or on the horse's day off. Traditionally, there is one groom to four horses and one hot walker to each groom. Nowadays this is not always the case because good help is hard to find, and finances tend to limit the staff trainers have. There are freelance hot walkers – meaning they are paid for each horse they walk and are not a regular member of the trainer's staff.

In general, hot walkers take the horse from the rider when he comes back from the track. If the horse gets a bath, the hot walker holds him as the groom bathes him. They walk the horse around the shed row until he is cool, usually for 20 to 30 minutes. If the horse is not training that day, the hot walker walks him "cold," meaning he did not get hot from training. Salaried hot walkers usually rake up and clean around the barn. They may fill hay nets and assist the groom when he needs an extra set of hands. Hot walkers also go to the races to assist the groom.

When a racehorse is walked, it is very different from the way show/pleasure horses lead. Think of leading pure power around. Horses are walked and handled outside of their stalls with the chain over their nose. Many bow their necks as they tow the walker around the shed row while others are as light as air. The hot walker keeps very close to the horse at his shoulder. When they are really feeling good or "sharp" as we call it, they may jig around the shed row. I have often said it's like leading a helium balloon around the barn.

There are mechanical hot walkers; they are quite common at some tracks. I cannot comment much on their use because I have not had a lot of experience with them. One machine that is used in Maryland is the Equiciser. It can be used as a hot walker, but most trainers use it to give the horse an easy day of training. Again, I do not have much experience with them, but from what I've seen most horses have fun in them.

Trainers

Please keep in mind when you come on the backstretch searching for your perfect horse, trainers are not in the business of selling horses. They tend to focus on their duties constantly because they are responsible for everything connected to the racehorse. The pressure a trainer carries is incredible. Horses are living, thinking creatures, so the trainer is in effect responsible for something that he cannot completely control. Every trainer has come across a horse possessed of incredible talent but they won't use it. If they do not want to race, there is little you can do. Imagine explaining this to the owner. Trainers make and are responsible for all decisions about the handling and care of the racehorse. Upon arrival at the barn each morning most trainers check each horse over. They look at them, feel their legs, and ask the groom if they ate breakfast or dinner from the night before. They make decisions about what the horse will do that day. Most trainers maintain a training chart, updating and adjusting the plan for the following day after training hours. Training instructions are subject to change even after the horse is on the track.

The trainer is responsible for educating the horse on how to be a racehorse and building the fitness needed to win races. He also makes decisions about all aspects of the horse's general welfare, including veterinary care. Remember, racehorses are athletes; this means their caretakers must spend a lot of time and energy making certain they are comfortable, healthy and able to perform.

The trainer also makes decisions about all aspects of the horse's general welfare, including veterinary care. Remember, racehorses are athletes; this means their caretakers must spend a lot of time and energy making certain they are comfortable and healthy and able to perform.

Trainers are responsible for selecting and entering horses in races. That may sound simple, but there are many types of races from which the trainer must choose. The following is a brief overview of the most common types of races. Claiming races are the most common races in Thoroughbred racing. The horse is entered for a specified price. I have seen them as low as $1,200 and as high as $100,000. At the end of such a race, if a claim has been made and the horse is sound, the horse has been sold and has a new owner. The horse is immediately taken to his new barn and the money is transferred into the seller's account. Maiden Claiming is the same as a claiming race, but all horses entered have never won a race.

Allowance races are the next step up in class. These are races where the amount of weight the horse carries and eligibility to enter are determined by conditions set by the racing secretary. Horses cannot be claimed from these races and the competition is much stiffer. A Maiden Special Weight is an Allowance race for maidens.

Stakes races are the next step up in class and considered more difficult than Allowance races. Horses cannot be claimed from these, either. There are different types of stakes races. The Overnight Stake is an informal stakes race. It is one way to give a horse a chance at "black type" – which is earned when a horse wins a Stake. "Black type" refers to the boldface print used in the sales catalogs provided at auctions of racing or breeding prospects to indicate horses that have won or placed in a stakes race. Such horses typically are worth more. Entries for stakes races close a specified number of hours before running. Horses are nominated for stakes races before entering; nominations may close far in advance.

An Ungraded Stake is not awarded Graded status by the governing committee. This committee examines and rates stakes races each year. Graded Stakes are the most important or prestigious races in North America. They are assigned grades (I, II, or III) based on the quality of previous winners and the race's influence on other races or championships. A Handicap is a race where the racing secretary or track handicapper assigns the weights to be carried in an attempt to make the competition more even. Typically, the most successful horses are assigned the most weight to carry.

There are conditions associated with all types of races. The purpose of conditions is to make races fair or "even" for horses by making it easier for a less experienced horse or one who has not been winning, to win a race. It may be as simple as assigning less weight to a horse who has not won a race this year. Common race conditions including limiting entries to horses who have not won two, three, or four races, meaning only horses in the designated category can enter. Races are also separated by age and sex. It is rare for geldings/stallions to run against fillies/mares. Two- and three-year-olds have races restricted to their age. The most common races are for three years old and up.

Most racehorses never win even one race. With each win, the odds of winning another race diminish exponentially. Once a horse is through the available conditions and must run in open company, meaning any horse can enter the race, he is much less desirable to the trainer and owner for it is less likely he will be able to make money or support his training bills.

Trainers must also communicate and socialize with their owners. A successful trainer is a good horseman and diplomat. Owners can be very passionate about their aspirations and desires and sometimes this can cause discord. Trainers also can be involved in selecting racing prospects, which means being educated in conformation and bloodlines. Time is spent attending sales and claiming races to study available horses. Some owners breed their own horses which can be a blessing or a curse.

Most trainers are present on race day. If the horse is late to the paddock the trainer is fined. A licensed trainer is required to saddle the horse in the paddock. When the trainer of record cannot be there, he has to arrange for another licensed trainer to saddle the horse.

There are large and small public racing stables that regularly take on new owners while others are private working for one owner. Each trainer has his own training style with a goal of winning races. A person who breeds and owns his own horses may become a trainer in order to train them. It is common for a groom or exercise rider to train his own horse. Jockeys who hold a trainer's license may only ride their own horses because it is considered a conflict for them to ride the horses of others.

Exercise Riders

These are all exercise riders at a Maryland Track.

The job of the exercise rider is different than that of the jockey. They gallop the horse in the morning so he will become fit enough to race and they educate the horse to be ridable for the jockey. Exercise riders typically ride with much longer stirrups than jockeys. They do not use their legs the same as the show ring rider, but racehorses have had legs on them. They teach the horse aids that are refined enough so the jockey can focus on riding the race. Another important job they do is to school each horse to the starting gate. A Thoroughbred must get a gate card, which means the horse is deemed to be educated and safe at the gate by the Head Starter.

Exercise riders come in all shapes and sizes and while it is possible to be too heavy or too tall, each trainer determines what his needs are. The average weight of an exercise rider is probably 125 pounds, but I have seen riders weighing up to 175 pounds at most tracks I have been to. Trainers may have a lighter rider or jockey breeze the horse, but the everyday guy generally weighs much more than a jockey.

Jockeys

Cloud's Honor wins at Philadelphia Park, Christopher VanHassel up.

Riding as a jockey is a highly specialized skill. The duty of the jockey is to guide the horse through traffic to win the race while executing the instructions of the trainer. Jockeys are responsible for countless decisions that must be made and executed in less than two minutes in most cases. The incredible strength and balance required of jockeys is basically so they can remain quiet and interfere with the horse as little as possible. Jockeys usually do not ride the horse on a daily basis. They usually breeze the horse (a timed workout at a specified distance) and ride the horse in races. It is common for a jockey to ride a horse for the first time in a race. This requires jockeys to be experts at reading horses to figure out how to ride them in a matter of minutes. Most race trackers know that a horse will tell you everything you need to know about him, if you listen. John (JK) Adams, a retired jockey who won more than 750 races, told me that "horses change from race to race so it's always necessary to assess the horse, even if you've ridden him regularly. What's important is how the horse is today." It's much the same in show riding. Olympian Jim Wofford has said to me on more than one occasion, "Don't ride yesterday's horse."

A successful jockey must know what to ask the horse and use only the exact aids to get that exact response. Asking for too much run at the wrong time requires the rider to take the horse back and can cost you the race. Ask for too little and the hole you want to go through closes before you get there. Jockeys must also study the other horses in the race and try to guess how it will unfold. They then try to position themselves and the horse to win the race. All plans are subject to change as the race unfolds.

Breaking from the gate is paramount to a good result. Many races are lost because of a poor start. The jockey must become an expert at staying in the center of the horse's motion at a time when there is sudden acceleration.

Even the warmup before the race makes a difference to the outcome of the race. Some horses take quite a bit of warming up. Others are on their toes when they step onto the racetrack; the jockey must decide whether to maintain that level of energy or try to relax the horse.

I could write a book just on race riding, but that is not the goal of this book. I will comment that both the rider and the horse are under considerable pressure during a race and the partnership they form is a very close one in most cases, even though it is developed in a short amount of time.

Veterinarians

Vets stop by the barn every day, creating an environment where the trainer can have any horse looked over should they have any concerns . I loved this because I galloped my own horses. If one of the horses hit the ground in a different way while galloping, I could have a vet take a look immediately. Often there are several vets in a practice giving the trainer the option of more than one opinion on the problem a horse may have. I know my horses received the best possible care in part due to the direct access to veterinary care.

Track vets have vast experience because they examine and treat so many horses. They usually have easy access to, and are very familiar with, state-of-the-art equipment for digital radiographs, ultrasound, and endoscopies, and so much more. Due to the sheer number of horses they work with, they are excellent diagnosticians and familiar with which treatments are most effective. In comparison, a farm vet has to drive from farm to farm, making it almost impossible for them to see or work with as many horses in a given day.

How they are ridden at the track

The rider who fosters the horse's spirit allows the horse to realize his true potential as a racehorse. The fundamentals of race riding are based on Classical Horsemanship because this is the most efficient way to communicate with a horse. There is nothing more natural to a Thoroughbred than to run. More than that, since Classical Horsemanship is based on the cause and effect of the aids, the horse doesn't have to think or reason, he only has to react. Since horses are reactive by nature, this aspect of race training is quite easy for them.

It is important to address some "myths" that seem to be persistent regarding racing and racehorses. The first is, racehorses do trot, or jog as we call it.

Racehorses know how to walk while being ridden. I have heard people unfamiliar with track practices say that racehorses are never ridden at the walk. That simply is untrue. They walk to and from the track for training. When the horse reaches the track, they usually walk for a prescribed distance, and then pick up a trot to warm up.

Riders at the track are good riders, duly licensed by the state and monitored for competence throughout their careers. They are very skilled in the art of riding racehorses which has some major differences from show riding. The fact that they don't look like show riders does not mean they lack the knowledge and skills to ride.

Racehorses do not run around like out-of-control wild animals. Their training is planned and has a format. For the most part, they do what they are asked to do. They have a lot of energy, which they are allowed to express to a point, but they focus on training or racing when asked.

All racehorses are not unsound. There are an awful lot of horses at the track and they all work most days. Racing asks more of a horse, so it only makes sense that you will see more soundness issues. Where else do you have a pool of horses that large training every day?

Color is irrelevant. People sometimes wonder if there is a color of horse that's more difficult to deal with. (Referring to the chestnut mare thing.) The answer is No. There was a time when I was getting on thirty horses a day. I galloped nice, nasty, kooky, smart, classy and crummy horses in every color, shape and size. It never occurred to me that I should avoid the chestnut fillies or any other color of horse. And every rider I asked about color indicating difficult or "hot" characteristics looked at me like I was an idiot.

There are many different riding styles at the track. The goal of the exercise rider is to carry out the trainer's instructions, not to look a certain way. Every horse has a different way of going. Riders ride behind other riders who may ride very differently than they do. It's the job of the rider to signal or "set up" the horse to do something and then stay out of his way allowing him to do his job. This approach is also frequently used in performance riding, such as setting a horse up for the jump and then leaving him be as he executes it. Or setting the horse up for a piaffe in dressage and then sitting quietly as the horse performs the movement. The rider at the track who bullies the horse into submission sacrifices the spirit of the horse in the process.

A pony rider takes a horse to post.

Balance is the foundation of correct exercise riding. Transference of the rider's body weight is the main means of communication. Pulling on the reins is an accelerator. Racehorses are on the forehand because it is faster, not because the riders do not know how to get a horse to use his rear end. Forward, as in forward going, is very important to the exercise rider. The lack of forwardness in any gait is a signal that something unpleasant is about to happen. The horse's withers and shoulders are the center of gravity at the gallop. The rider moves in sync with the horse's motion. When the rider is stiff the horse becomes uncomfortable, due to the extra work it creates for both the rider and horse. Ideally, the rider keeps his balance in the two-point position (the two points being the rider's two feet) over the shoulders during the gallop. Exercise riders and jockeys balance their weight over their feet; they do not grip with their legs. To maintain a straight back the abdominal muscles are pushed out rather than in. The knees of the rider absorb most of the shock. All of the joints are absorbing some of the shock allowing the rider to be strong but flexible, not rigid. The rider's head and upper body remain still. When the rider's position is correct and balanced, he will be thrown back into the tack rather than pitched off when the horse makes an unexpected move such as a spook or stumble.

Getting out of balance by being in front of the motion of a racehorse is not a good place to be. If the horse stumbles or takes a bad step, the rider risks a dirt bath. There is one time when a rider might be a little ahead of the motion, and that is coming out of the starting gate. It does have its cost at times. In an attempt to free up the horse to get out of the gate, the rider is forward over the horse's shoulders. He's ahead of the motion to facilitate a quick departure. During that moment if the ground breaks away or the horse stumbles the jockey can pay the price by coming off.

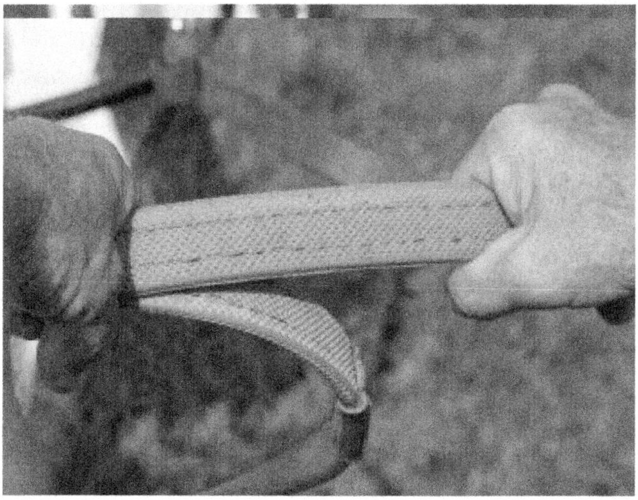

Half Cross

The "home position" of the exercise rider's hands has the knuckles of each hand pressed flat into either side of the withers.

This is one of the most difficult things for the show rider to master when first learning to gallop racehorses. The wide reins used at the track are held in a full or half cross. These techniques allow the rider to let the horse pull on himself instead of directly on the rider. A full cross is when both reins are held together in both hands making a bridge to be placed on either side of the withers.

The hands are held the same width as the bit. This cross is for the toughies. Most riders prefer the half cross. The left rein is held in the left hand, crosses the withers and held in the right hand. The right rein is held only in the right hand. This can be done in reverse, too. Hands are kept on either side of the withers the same as with the full cross.

A good rider gives the racehorse a stable place to pull. The rider lets the horse take hold of the bit; he never initiates the pulling contact. The same hold is maintained throughout the training session. This means the reins are not shortened, lengthened or pulled on during the ride. To change the hold means asking the horse to go faster. In races, if the jockey changes his hold, it is to tell the horse to go. Keep this in mind when riding your newly retired racer. Each horse pulls differently, some pull very hard and others not so much. When a horse pulls hard, it does not mean he's going to run off. Horses will pull harder when they are sharp, excited or before they break off to breeze. It is desirable for the horse to be on that "edge" because the jockey will have only to whisper "go." Tough horses are "held" to a slow gallop by keeping the rider's hands down and shifting the weight behind the vertical for the entire ride. The rider must remain completely still during this time. This requires great body, core and leg strength.

Stirrup length varies according to the needs of the rider and his individual riding style. Some exercise riders ride long and others short. Still others, and probably the best, adjust the length of the stirrup for that particular horse and the instructions of the day. The better riders do not support their weight on the horse's mouth, no matter what the length of their stirrups. Most people ride the shortest when they are breezing. Two exceptions are when teaching babies to breeze and when riding them the first few times on the rail. The tougher the horse is to gallop, the shorter the stirrup length must be because the shorter the stirrups are, the more leverage the rider has to hold the horse. If the horse is unpredictable and/or performing athletic feats the rider has to ride longer in order to stay on. "The longer you ride, the longer you ride," is the old timer's adage. This is true and most of the experienced riders ride longer than an outsider would expect. It is easier to ride most horses longer and to avoid supporting oneself on the horse's mouth while remaining balanced and in the center of the motion. Riding those tough, bad actors takes a tremendous amount of strength when the rider doesn't have the leverage of the shorter stirrups as a tool. In the end though, it's good to stay on. Jockeys always ride really short, and that is one reason a lead pony escorts them to the starting gate.

Understanding how riders at the track stop and slow racehorses is helpful in retraining them. Many racehorses will slow and even stop by pulling on the yoke. This is not intentionally taught to them but is a result of being ridden with one. Standing up in the stirrups drops the rider's weight into the center of the horse. This is the equivalent to applying the brakes for the horse. Shifting of the rider's weight behind the vertical is the exercise rider's use of the "seat." It is the race rider's half halt. The beginning of the slowdown is well in advance of the desired place to stop. An example of this is when the

The rider in front is holding her horse and the other rider is allowing her horse to run. Perhaps the trainer instructed them to stay together and the horse behind is not keeping up, so the horse on the lead must be held.

rider is pulling up after a gallop. In a normal gallop, the horse is prepared or signaled a quarter of a mile or more before he is to pull up. When watching a race, notice the horses pull up and head home on the other side of the track after passing the finish line. As the rider begins to pull the horse up, his hold is softened and body weight is shifted behind the vertical as he straightens his knees. The rhythm of the rider's body slows, encouraging the horse to slow the rhythm of his gallop. Both hands are usually kept down on the withers, although with some horses the reins may be lifted and lowered several times, not pulled back, simply lifted and lowered.

Racehorses must learn how to gallop. The main difference between galloping and just running is determined by the length and amount of strides the horse takes. To increase the speed at the gallop means the horse must open or extend his stride. Running means the horse is taking more steps more rapidly to increase his speed and cover more ground instead of opening his stride. These extra steps tire the horse quickly.

There are different gears within the gallop gait. The term hobby horse refers to the slowest type of gallop speed or "gear." It is just as it sounds, almost a rocking slow motion canter; a regular trot is much faster. In reality it's not a gallop at all—it's a canter on the forehand. This speed is usually uncomfortable for the fit racehorse and hard on the rider because most horses really pull when held this slow. Next is the medium or regular gallop. This is the normal galloping speed of most horses and for most trainers. For those eventers out there, a normal gallop for a horse is the Training Level speed for cross country.

The next "gear" is the strong gallop which is a forward, comfortable gait. The rider usually doesn't have to work very hard to maintain this speed, except on the horses that like to pull or, of course, lazy horses. Next is the two-minute lick, which means one mile is galloped in two minutes. It is the "gear" just below a breeze. This speed and breezing are used to put air into the horse, not necessarily to build muscle. Once the horse is racing fit, these workouts are scheduled carefully in relation to race days. Two-minute licks usually cause the horse to "sharpen" or to "get on his toes." Again, for eventers this speed is just a tad faster than Advanced cross-country speed— so those guys are moving!

Breezing is the fastest speed in the morning, and most often it's a bit slower than racing speed. Many consider this a different gait than galloping and I have to agree. Racetrackers do not consider it a gallop at all. It is the point where the rider ceases to feel the hoof beats any longer. I liken it to space movies where the spaceship enters warp speed. The sensation is smooth and effortless on a good horse. You usually do not hear anything except for the horse's breath and your own. It is a timed workout; used to prep horses for races or for getting them fit. A breeze can be easy or strong. To get a young horse fit, he can be breezed at 5-to-7-day intervals. To prepare a horse for a race he is typically breezed 2 to 3 days before that race. However, each trainer has his own training style and each horse *is* an individual.

When galloping or jogging in company, the exercise rider may stay just a nose off the other horse. This helps most horses to relax. Jockeys do this in races to get the horse to relax and save himself for the end run. The rider's body must remain supple and soft while exerting tremendous strength at the same time. This is worth remembering when retraining your OTTB to trail ride or hack with other horses. Keep it in mind when you venture out cross country on your new retired racehorse. Putting the uptight horse just a nose off of a calmer one may be just the way to get him to relax.

Lead changes are introduced to racehorses early in their training. The racehorse travels on the inside or left lead in the turns and on the outside or right lead on the straights of the racetrack. Riders ask for a lead change by stepping into the stirrup of the lead they want, not by use of their leg or reins. I want to stress here, they do not lean. They are still in the middle of the motion. If anything they are a tad more to the outside when they step into the inside stirrup. If you think about it, it's the only way jockeys could possibly ask for a lead since they ride so short and their legs are not really in contact with the horse's side. The horse changes leads as a reaction to this aid which is an efficient way to ask for the change. The changes must be smooth and effortless. All tracks are basically the same, so the horse learns through habit to change. They also learn that it's easier to work if they change leads in these spots. Often the jockey doesn't have to ask the horse to change at all once it becomes a habit. You really do not need to teach your OTTB to change leads since he regularly does it at the track. You only have to remodel the system for asking for the change. The biggest hurdle is that the horse is used to having momentum when he changes. Momentum does not mean speed; it means moving forward impelled by the horse's velocity and strength so you'll need to develop some topline to make up for the loss of that momentum before you ask.

Most horses are ridden to and from the track with loose or gentle rein contact. The reins are picked up when preparing to trot or gallop. "On the bit" means the horse is in a frame and listening to our aids, similar to the riding horse's "on the bit." The major difference is at the track the horse is on the forehand.

Thoroughbred racehorses are accustomed to being asked, not

Home position of the hands is on the withers.

forced to do things. They are by nature very generous. Most exercise riders and jockeys are very good at leaving horses alone. One difference in riding the racehorse worth mentioning is the way an exercise rider or jockey rewards the horse for responding to a request. In show and pleasure horses it is customary to soften the reins when the horse obeys. This is the way the horse is rewarded. In racing the reward is more that the rider stays the same. We do soften or relax our joints with the motion. This is a difficult thing to explain, but basically if we ask the horse to pick the pace up, we do it by relaxing our hold and our body and then stay that way to reward. The horse then picks up the bit as he picks up the pace and we stay the same, giving him a stable place to take hold.

When the horse enters training for another discipline, take care not to overemphasize the aids because the horse may become annoyed or upset at what he perceives as nagging. In racing, a little aid goes a very long way. Most exercise riders have an evolved degree of subtlety which is a necessity on a high-performance horse. This subtlety allows a jockey to ride the horse with his irons so short, because it takes so little to get the horse to respond. Some of the perceived "craziness" of off-track Thoroughbreds comes from the fact that their new riders do not realize how little they have to do to get a response from these wonderful athletes. The more fit the horse, the more responsive and touchier he is. With time the horse will learn to accept stronger aids or better yet the rider will learn to be more accurate and subtle with his aids. This is one reason you may want to let the horse down before your retraining begins.

Tack

As in all equine disciplines there is specialized tack to help the rider do the job. Racing is no exception. There are specialized bridles, saddles and tack. There are preferred bits and other equipment.

Some horses work and even race with no noseband at all. A common noseband used at the track is the figure 8 which is used to discourage the horse from opening his mouth. When a horse opens his mouth he is resisting the bit, but worse than that, he can bite or even swallow his tongue. Any movement of the tongue can impede airflow and the racehorse needs all the air he can get while running.

The reins are one inch wide and covered in textured rubber. Thin reins would cut into the rider's hands. Thick reins make it easier to keep hold of the reins and maintain a consistent rein length which is imperative in galloping racehorses.

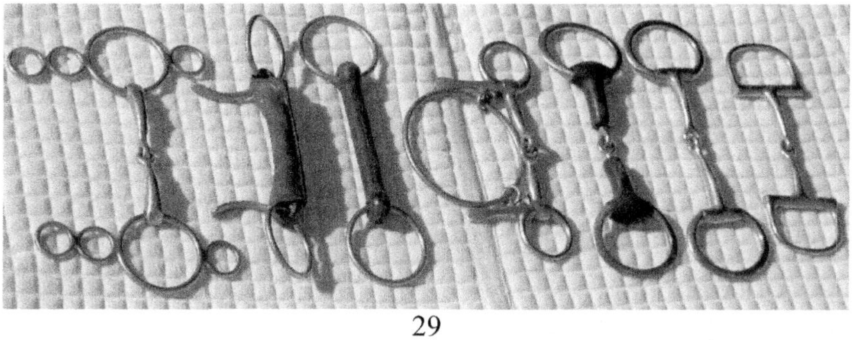

Pictured are some of the most commonly used bits at the track. Each trainer has his own training beliefs and those pictured do not represent every bit you will find at the track.

Working left to right, the first bit is commonly called an elevator bit and is not used often at the track. It is used on horses that are tough to hold. Usually, trainers have tried other options before resorting to this bit.

The next bit is a leather prong bit. The prongs are used to exert pressure on the side of the mouth, assisting the rider when the horse won't steer or to break the hold if the horse is one who likes to grab the bit and go. When the prongs are not in play, it's just a fat, straight, loose ring bit.

The next bit is a straight, loose ring rubber bit, sometimes called a dog bone. It is commonly used on babies and sensitive mouthed horses. Straight bits are good for horses with breathing issues.

The next is the ring bit, another snaffle type bit. It can have side prongs to help with steering. The horse plays with the ring and this encourages acceptance of the bit. Some people outside racing think it is a harsh bit, most likely because it has a complicated look but it functions like a snaffle bit.

The next two are egg butt snaffle bits. The name refers to the shape of the bit's cheek pieces. They are the favorite of lots of trainers and riders. They are kind bits that are hinged so they won't pinch the side of the mouth. The first egg butt is a rubber one and is a very mild bit. The next is a standard thickness and made of steel.

Probably the most common bit is the last one pictured. It is a traditional racing bit and is called a D-bit. It's a snaffle style bit with D-shaped cheek pieces for extra control on the sides for aid with steering. It comes in many thicknesses.

Exercise saddles have a "half" tree making them smaller and lighter than saddles used in other disciplines. They weigh on average 7 pounds and the tree is only in the front of the saddle. The saddles used for racing are even smaller and lighter. They weigh from 14 ounces for a "small" to 2 pounds for a "large." They are meant to be used on the horse for a very short period of time and intended to save weight. Race saddles are held in place by a girth and an overgirth.

Both German martingales and draw reins are used at the track. Their use is usually reserved for special circumstances when the horse is either too tough to hold any other way, or to help with a star gazer (horse who gallops and trains with their head extremely high). I would like to note that I believe rather than applying these gizmos, the reason the horse is carrying himself this way should be identified and then addressed. Once a horse can be controlled with either draw reins or the German martingale, it adds a layer of difficulty in transitioning him to traveling in a correct body shape without them.

The yoke or neck strap, as it's called in other disciplines, is a strap that goes around the neck in front of the saddle with another strap between the legs attaching to the girth. In racing, the yoke is sometimes used to clip rings to.

Rings are similar to a running martingale. They have a rectangular piece of leather or nylon with a clip to attach it to the yoke. There are two rings on the other two corners for the reins go through. The main reason for a yoke is for safety. The yoke is the exercise rider's best friend. Most riders at the track will have a finger or two in it at all times. This habit prevents harsh hand movements which happen when the horse makes a sudden move and the rider is caught unprepared. This habit may save the rider's life on a horse that rears as it keeps the rider from pulling back on the horse's mouth, which can result in pulling the horse over in the process.

The use of blinkers is common in racing. They can help a horse to focus on the job at hand. Some horses are worried about the horses around them and blinkers help the horse deal with that. There are also horses that are worried about the rider and what he is doing; blinkers can help with that as well. Some nervous horses go well in them, but others become more nervous. The only real way to know if they will be helpful is to try them. The blinker cups come in different sizes from full cups to just slight cups. There are also protective "bubbles" that are for eye protection. There is even a cup that blacks out one eye called a "run out" blinker for horses that bolt in one direction which is very dangerous. The horse must be okayed from the starting gate to race in blinkers and given a blinker card.

How racehorses are trained

Each trainer has his own beliefs and training schedule, but I will attempt to outline what racehorses do at the track. Please understand there are lots of ways to get a horse race ready, but there are some basic instructions that I got regularly as an exercise rider from lots of different trainers.

Most tracks are a mile or 1-1/16 miles, although there are some that are 5/8 and a few that are 1-1/8. Belmont Park in Elmont, NY is the longest track in America at 1-1/2 miles. A typical day of training for a baby racehorse (new to the track, usually two years old), is to walk to the track, with another baby or a pony and go straight off

This horse gallops in blinkers and a shadow roll.

once around. Straight off is called the right way. It is the counterclockwise direction of the track in America. You might jog off an eighth of a mile or more before picking up a gallop.

For most other racehorses, you first "back them up" or what racetrackers call "jogging the wrong way" for a quarter to a half mile, stop, turn in and stand, then gallop around the track once. The jog is intended to warm the horse up. Riders may jog back to the wire, gallop around the track past the wire and pull up at the 5/8 or 1/2 mile pole. It's never good to pull up before the wire because the horse needs to think GO in the stretch, not HO. At the end of the gallop the horse stands in again. During this time, the horse and rider watch the other horses train as they gallop and jog by.

In most cases, seasoned horses gallop anywhere from a mile to a mile and a half per day. Every trainer has his own ideas. Some like to see their horses hobby horse while others like to see them gallop along. Some trainers prefer their horses jog every day except on breeze and race days. Training by jogging sharpens the horse to stellar proportions and it's usually miserable to ride them, but oftentimes they race well. Most of these horses are older and have raced, so fitness is not the issue. This type of training will also freshen horses who need a break.

The furthest distance most horses at the track gallop is two miles. You will rarely ever see one train further on purpose. When I trained horses, I liked to go two miles with my horses two weeks before their first race going long (a race at a mile or over). I would do the first mile at a normal pace, pick it up on the second mile and breeze the last quarter mile. I felt this was better for them than breezing a full mile. Horses that have not run may do two miles once a week, but probably not more often than that.

Breezing develops the racing speed and air in a racehorse. When getting a horse fit, a normal space between breezes is five days, with a day off after the breeze. Horses who are racing usually breeze a few days before they race to put air in them since they are already fit. With babies, you would start out doing 1/8 mile to the wire, meaning the end of the breeze is at the wire. Then breeze 1/4 mile once or twice with 3/8 mile being the first "formal" workout where the time counts. A time of .40 or .38 would be a good easy 3/8 workout. Older seasoned horses do .37, smoking is .36. Gradually every 5 to 7 days the distance is lengthened. I used to do two of each, meaning 3/8 mile and seven days later another 3/8 mile, but galloping out a strong 1/2 mile to set up for the first 1/2 mile breeze. 3/8 to 5/8 mile work outs are the most common distances. Once the horse is fit, breezes are used to prep horses for races. In general, short distance workouts are good for sprinters, longer workouts of over a half mile are good for distance horses.

Trainers may have riders shedrow a horse. Race barns are constructed with a shed row that goes around the block of stalls. "Shedrowing" means the riders walk or jog the horse around the barn for a specified amount of time, usually 20 to 25 minutes. There is so much to explain, this just scratches the surface of training the racehorse.

There are rules riders must follow when riding on the track. Every track I have galloped at has the same basic rules with only minor differences. Horses gallop the "right way" or counterclockwise on the racetrack. The inside rail is reserved for the fastest speeds, which are breezing speeds. As you move out from the inside rail the galloping speeds become slower. Where possible, horses pass to the inside, and it's wise to say "coming by" to the rider you are passing.

The outside rail is reserved for jogging and traveling in the clockwise direction. It is called "the wrong way" so if a trainer tells you to go 2 miles the wrong way, they are telling you to jog the horse. No galloping is allowed when you go the wrong way. Many young or green horses are frightened the first few times they jog the "wrong way." With time they become accustomed to the other horses who are galloping toward them. Remember, these are the horses galloping the slowest.

The Starting Gate

A fair start to the race.

Thoroughbred horses must be educated on how to break from the gate. Each track employs a group of highly experienced men and women who handle the horses at the gate. The person who starts each race is the Starter and all of the other handlers are Assistant Starters. A horse must have a gate card before he can race. To receive this card, the Starter must okay the horse for breaking from the gate.

During the races, the assistant starters load the horses and hold each horse's head until the starter presses the button that causes the front doors of the starting gate to open. The goal is to have a clean and fair start to the race for all of the horses. Each assistant starter must have each horse standing squarely and focused on breaking as the gate opens. These people are committed to the safety of the horses, jockeys and exercise riders.

The gate crew also works with the horses in the morning teaching them how behave in the starting gate. They want each horse to be comfortable and confident there. Schooling in the gate occurs at different points of the horse's training depending on the trainer's judgment. Many riders prefer that it begin before the horse is too fit as the starting gate can be a very intimidating and exciting place. Every Thoroughbred racehorse is ridden into this small area and required to stand and wait to break from the gate. Racehorses are not crazy, if they were, flat races could not begin this way.

When you purchase a horse off the track, you are getting a horse capable of incredible obedience during stressful times, such as the start of a race. Think about racehorses in the paddock before a race. They are at peak fitness and know the race is coming. It is an exciting time for them. Yet in most cases, they walk around quietly until it is time to go to the track. You do have your dancers but they too stay with their handler. Your retired racehorse is capable of behaving the same way in other stressful situations with proper handling. □

3 YOU'RE READY TO START LOOKING

You should have an idea of the kind of horse you will be looking for. This will save you and the sellers a lot of time but more importantly, it will keep you on track to finding the best horse for your needs. There are so many types of Thoroughbreds. It's important to have an idea of the type of temperament, physical condition, and flaws you are willing to accept. What are you going to be doing with your new horse? How much horse do you need? Having too much horse isn't necessarily a blessing. Often people think that very talented horses will be easier to train and will progress faster. The opposite is true. When a horse is extremely athletic and talented, they are going to need more training in order for us to be able to manage and direct all that they are. They need more aids developed by more training or in simpler terms, they need more buttons to push. The more athletic the horse, the more athletic the rider must be. The reactions of an athletic horse are quicker and this kind of horse's resistance is usually more effective.

While it can be easier to push a talented horse to do things faster, without a proper foundation, this approach will usually run its course and we will be left with a badly trained, difficult horse. We will be lucky if he isn't physically injured by being pushed. Pushing horses past their training will use them up and scrub off their brilliance.

You also need to consider the cost of care and retraining, both routine and unexpected veterinary costs and what you will do if the horse turns out to be unable to fulfill your requirements. In addition, I encourage everyone to plan for the horse's retirement from the day they take the horse on. It should be no surprise that the horse will need to retire one day. If everyone provided for that ahead of time, the job of rescues like mine would be much easier. Horses will give their all to you. You owe it to them to consider the responsibility of owning one very carefully.

Some trainers will sell their horses on their own, only sending them to an aftercare organization if they can't move them. You can check horse journal classifieds, Facebook and the internet to find someone that represents trainers on the backstretch. Please keep in mind, they are horse dealers who work with trainers, buying some of their horses and then reselling them for a profit. You can get a good horse from them but be mindful they are working to make a profit; they are not a charity.

You may want to go to the track yourself. If you decide to try this, here are some tips to help you be prepared. Take identification, as you will be asked for it by security. Take a camera, pen and paper for notes about the horses you see. Record the name of the horse and trainer, barn number where they are located, contact information, and the vet they use. Note any observations before moving on to the next horse. Keep in mind that most tracks do not allow dogs. One of the most powerful negotiating points for most trainers is knowing when you plan to take the horse. Generally, the sooner the better. If you want a great price, arrive at the track prepared to buy. If you're willing to take the horse that day, many sellers will be much more willing to negotiate. Bring your horse trailer, just in case, but do not feel pressure to fill it if you do not see the horse of your dreams.

There are different ways to get on the track when looking for a horse. If you're the outgoing type, you can go to the Secretary's office on race days. There are always trainers hanging out in the Secretary's Office during the races. They may have horses ready to retire or know who does. In addition, the people who work there may be able to put you in contact with someone who'll get you on the backstretch. They may even know who has horses to sell or rehome. Another option is to show up at the entrance gate to the backstretch early in the morning. Ask the guards to announce you're there looking to buy. This can be an uncertain, though many times effective way to get connected. Most tracks require a trainer or owner sign for and be responsible for an unlicensed person for the day.

There are different ways to get on the track when looking for a horse. If you're the outgoing type, you can go to the Secretary's office on race days. There are always trainers hanging out in the Secretary's Office during the races. They may have horses ready to retire or know who does. In addition, the people who work there may be able to put you in contact with someone who'll get you on the backstretch. They may even know who has horses to sell or rehome. Another option is to show up at the entrance gate to the backstretch early in the morning. Ask the guards to announce you're there looking to buy. This can be an uncertain, though many times effective way to get connected. Most tracks require a trainer or owner sign for and be responsible for an unlicensed person for the day.

When in a barn, stay on the inside of the shedrow, by the stalls, which will put you on the left side of the horses as they walk around the shed row. Never stand on the "outside" or right side of a racehorse. This is standard protocol and the handler is able to keep others out of harm's way more effectively when all are on the same side of the horse. It's the left because most horses are left "handed." Remember this rule applies to horses who are being hosed, groomed or otherwise worked on. Horses have the right of way at all times. This means you do not walk in front of them and never run unless you are escaping danger and there's no other way to get to safety. Do not use flashes when taking pictures. Plastic bags or other noisy things are not welcome.

While watching horses on the track, do not stand close to the rail, for this can frighten young horses. It is advisable to stand in the open so the horses can easily identify that you are a human, not something stalking them preparing to pounce. Many times a rider will sound rude when telling you to get out of his way. Loud and mean is more likely to get an immediate response. He is not mad at you. Later, you will find the same rider to be polite and friendly. This is a result of the high potential for disaster when things go wrong on the track. There's a lot of adrenaline around the racetrack and it's not just in the horses.

My advice in finding the right horse is to trust your first impression of each horse. If you're walking away trying to convince yourself he's the right one, he most likely is not. It should be similar to love at first sight. Also, be objective about the good and the bad in every horse. It's too easy to fall in love with a horse and miss the things that may be an issue later on. You may even miss great potential when you only look for the imperfections. Remember, there are no perfect horses, just the perfect horse for you!

Assessing the temperament and movement of horses you're considering is not so easy if you are not used to horses in race training. A seemingly high-strung individual could in fact be a teddy bear once let down on a farm. When evaluating movement, take into account that racehorses are shod for speed, not quality of movement. Keep in mind that training style and physical issues can affect both movement and temperament. If the horse is sore he may be more wound up and tight in his body making it difficult to assess either. Both feeding programs and soreness can make a horse sour, depressed or aggressive. Veterinary treatments also may be an issue. When watching the horse train, ask if the horse was off the day before—Sunday is the common day off. If off the day before, the horse is likely to be much higher than normal. In this case, where possible come and see the horse train the next day and note how much he calms down. This would be indicative of how he will let down when you get him home.

Lots of horses at the track move in a "hocky" sort of way. They pick their hocks up higher and put them down quickly when jogging (trotting). I see this often in the horses that come to my farm and I don't worry about it at all if they move evenly "hocky." I'm not sure why they move this way, whether it's the deeper footing, the way they're trained or the fact that their backs are generally tighter than show horses. I can tell you that it normally subsides in the first two weeks they are on the farm letting down. If I already think the horse is a decent mover, I expect it to improve dramatically as he lets down.

Some prospects can be a great deal because they are not "suitable" to the majority of buyers. Colts are the most "undesirable" sex of horse for most people, with geldings the most popular. If you are willing to consider a colt, you will have less competition for some very nice horses. It's neither hard nor expensive to turn a colt into a gelding. You may be able to negotiate a deal where the colt is gelded before you take him. Most horses need a letdown period anyway and by the time your new horse is ready to begin training, the "colt" can be out of him. Two-year-olds are another overlooked group. They will grow and develop into the very horse you are looking for. It's not unusual to take a year or more to get them show ready anyway. During this time, you can form a solid relationship with the horse. They have been lightly raced and are generally easier to transition.

The most common types of racing careers a horse can have are outlined in the next few pages. I'll be generalizing because there are too many variables to list them all. Most of the horses you come across will fall into one of these categories..

The Unraced Thoroughbred

Unraced seems really good and many times it is, but it can also be a bad sign if it's due to an unsoundness of a permanent nature. The horse could have poor conformation and may not have held up to the stresses of race training. Less than perfect management while raising the horse may result in negative physical issues. There are other instances where the horse may have sustained an injury that will heal, but it's been decided it's too late in the game to get him to the races. Remember, racing is a time-limited venture. There is much more development time in show and pleasure pursuits. Horses get heavier as they get older and many trainers, myself included, recognize the odds are against getting an older horse to the races successfully. There are always exceptional circumstances, but the more mass the horse carries, the bigger the chance of injury and the harder they have to work to go fast. It's easy to ask why the horse never raced and get a vet to do a basic pre-purchase exam to confirm the explanation.

In other cases, a horse may not have demonstrated talent or desire in training and the trainer/owner felt it better to move on to other prospects. Usually, the horse has had enough training to be well broke but has not yet trained hard enough to develop any wear and tear. It is important to note that lots of "untalented" racehorses have both the ability and athleticism needed for other disciplines; they just do not have the competitive desire to be successful racehorses. Often this leads to a quieter, cooperative temperament which is a great quality in a show/pleasure horse.

Another all-too-common reason for not racing a horse is that money is not available to get a horse to the races. Lots of people breed horses not realizing how expensive it is to get a horse to the races. This can lead to a horse ending up in the show or pleasure ring with someone else, instead of on the track. Expenses add up in racing. There are training fees, the vet, farrier and many other expenses on top. Before a horse even gets to the track they have to be taught the basics of being handled and ridden. Racehorses are an expensive luxury. It's possible to have horses in training and then have financial issues that result in not being able to afford to continue on. Sometimes this happens when a horse is injured in training. If the injury requires a lengthy recovery period, followed by an even longer time to train and build fitness before racing, it may make more sense financially to retire the horse. Often horses that are not raced for financial reasons are sold within racing, but they also can be a good value for the show/pleasure world.

There is the occasional horse with a horrible temperament. He just doesn't fit into the training program of racehorses. These horses are easy to spot and likely won't make a good show horse either. Fortunately, most Thoroughbreds want to please and this is a very uncommon occurrence.

The Lightly Raced Thoroughbred

Don't shy away from a horse that only ran a few times and is now for sale. It is likely the trainer already knows the horse lacks talent but races the horse to convince the owner. The horse may have shown talent in the morning but didn't assert himself during the race. They call them "morning glories," and they are the most frustrating horses to train. These horses have the talent, but lack the mentality to go with racing. They often are the best show prospects. Another common reason for only a few starts is that good trainers will stop a horse because they can see the horse is not going to stand up to the rigors of racing. These horses will be suitable for almost anything else, including jumping. Racing asks more of a horse than any other discipline I know of, and at a younger age. It speaks to a trainer's integrity and judgment that he stops a horse long before he is injured, saving the horse and the money of the owner, too. Consequently, these horses are often a great buy. It's a safe bet that this horse has been handled correctly all along.

The War Horse

There are horses that have long racing careers and retire sound. Do not eliminate a horse from consideration simply because he's raced a lot. This is a tough horse that's been soundness tested. He has the class to handle the stress and pressure of racing. Usually, these horses are very smart and have the competitive edge and pride everyone is looking for. Horses that try for their humans can be counted on and that's a special quality.

Their Racing History

Once the horse races, his history is publicly documented. Comprehensive records are kept of each race a horse runs. When you start considering horses, it is a good idea to learn how to use some of these tools. You can gain insight into the type of horse he is, the time he's had off during his career, and where he's been. Plus, it's fun. You may be able to find videos of his races.

It's very easy to access a Thoroughbred racehorse's history. You can get his or her history through one of many services either free or for a fee.

The Daily Racing Form is the "Bible" of Thoroughbred horsemen. They provide the latest news in racing and past performances of horses entered that day. You can find tutorials on how to read the form on Youtube.

Equibase, an offshoot of the DRF, is one place you can go to get the entire racing history of your horse. You can get the past performances of every race he ever ran, or the charts, which are results of each race with descriptive comments. You can also access his breeding if that's of interest to you.

Brisnet is yet another service that offers similar information for a fee.

The Jockey Club is the registry of Thoroughbreds, but it has many other functions. It can be helpful in a myriad of ways in finding information on a Thoroughbred. Their staff is very helpful if you contact them with almost any questions you may have.

Pedigree Query will give you basic information about your horse's breeding at no charge. There are others, if you search around on the internet.

Next I will discuss a horse's racing history as it applies to the needs of someone looking for a show/pleasure prospect. This information is used by handicappers to bet, and trainers and owners to strategize their races. They also use it for shopping for horses to claim. The show and pleasure horse shopper uses it to get clues about how the horse has been trained, where he's been and how much time he's had off along with clues to why he had that time.

The past performances or the charts give you a description of each race a horse ran. I am going to stick with the pp's, because that's what I pull on a prospect. You get the date he ran, the track, weather, distance of race, jockey, trainer, owner, where he was at different points in the race, where he finished, his most recent breezes, age, color, dam, sire, where he was bred, price paid if purchased at a sale, stud fee, lifetime earnings, earnings by year and what surfaces he made the money on. You also get surface condition for each race, meaning whether the race was on dirt, turf, or synthetic and whether the track was wet or dry. They even publish whether he had front bandages, blinkers, Lasix or adjunct medication. You get a lot of information, but what do you do with it?

First, let me state there are no hard and fast rules to follow. The racing history will provide clues that are helpful, and maybe give you some questions to ask the person selling or rehoming the horse. Let's begin by talking about racing style. Every horse has a preferred way of running. This is determined by the horse and really cannot be changed very much. Trainers know this and spend time learning the horse's style and finding him the appropriate races. Some horses like to run long, meaning their races are a longer distance. Others prefer short races; these are the sprinters.

Body types suggest a preferred distance, but there are always exceptions. Sprinters tend to be more compact, while distance runners generally are bigger and cover more ground. Whatever the horse's best distance, he will have a running style. Knowing running style can help with retraining. Some horses like to lead the entire race while others like to drop back and do all of the running at the end. Still other horses like to sit a few lengths off the lead and then make their move. It all depends on how the horse will best relax in the race so he has the most energy to try to win at the end. Horses are trained according to their racing style. Keep that in mind on your first trail rides; you may be able to help your horse relax just by where you put him among the other horses, based on how he liked to race. Front end horses and sprinters tend to be less patient. Distance horses have more stamina. Think about those first trail rides and how you can better relax the horse just by where you put him among the other horses. A sprinter may take more warming up to instill patience in him. Keep these characteristics in mind when working with your new friend.

Gaps in a horse's racing history can mean a rest period or an injury. There are clues in the amount of time off, time of year and location of the track. If you get to know the trainer's style, you may find he gives all 2-year-olds off about that amount of time. When you see an extended time between two races, bear in mind that's the rest period (whether for injury recovery or just time off) plus the time it took to get the horse race ready again. Gaps in a horse's form when they are younger do not necessarily worry me. Sometimes the older guy gets time off just because he's been there a while and needed to be freshened. Six months off is maybe four months rest and sixty days to regain fitness. A month between races is nothing; they probably couldn't find a race. Even two months could be explained for the same reason. It is expected that young horses will suffer from respiratory illness more often, just like children when they first attend school. Many young horses have shin soreness requiring time off. Grass horses in the mid-Atlantic area may spend the winter on vacation because there is no turf racing.

A horse that's had a lot of trainers and lived at many tracks and is not nervous is a well-adjusted individual. When possible, ask the trainer, groom and exercise rider questions about the horse. How is he for the blacksmith and vet? What is he like to ride? How is he to handle at the races?

Health and Soundness Issues Overview

While you make your rounds looking for a horse, you should be familiar with some of the more common health and soundness issues. While it is advisable to have a pre purchase exam done on any horse you're interested in, it's also good to have a basic understanding of some of the issues you may encounter.

Dr. Carol Swandby, a long time Maryland horseman and veterinarian, has graciously given a brief overview of some of the most common veterinary topics you will likely come across in your search for a new horse.

"Bleeding (exercise-induced pulmonary hemorrhage or EIPH) is not an issue for the non-racing athlete. I am never concerned that a horse is on Lasix." Lasix is an anti-bleeding medication administered to some racehorses.

Breathing problems and the sounds they make: "If the horse is a roarer (left laryngeal hemiplegia) there may be an issue if you plan to show in the hunter division. Upper airway noises are considered faults. Check with your show organization. If the horse does make a noise, have an endoscopic exam performed to determine the cause."

Osselets is a slang term for any enlargement of the front ankles. They represent overexertion - stretching of the soft tissues. Once the horse has them it is a permanent blemish.

Splints on a Thoroughbred are not a concern for future disciplines. Splints will not become a source of lameness unless the horse is longed frequently and/or for an extended period of time.

Ringbone is generally not seen in the racing Thoroughbred. This is a condition of older horses.

Chips in any joint may be a problem in the future. If the chips are new, they can be removed with a good prognosis for riding and performance. You must have x-rays done and submit them to a surgeon for their opinion on prognosis. Left in, chips are always associated with degenerative joint disease. Horses with chips can be serviceably sound for many years as trail horses, companions and broodmares. Horses with chips should not be considered for resale projects as they will not "pass" a ppe.

Bows are any injury to the superficial digital flexor tendon. It is an injury associated with fatigue. The only disciplines that an old bow may be a problem for are combined training where there is a lot of galloping, and steeplechasing.

Capped hocks and elbows are strictly cosmetic and not associated with lameness.

A healthy suspensory is necessary in dressage, show jumping, and most competitive disciplines. Suspensory ligament injuries can be associated with broken splint bones and/or sesamoids. When considering a horse with this issue have an ultrasound exam and radiographs taken.

String halt – uncommon in the young Thoroughbred.

Hock problems are usually associated with OCD (osteochondritis dissecans). Racing Thoroughbreds do not jump, so degeneration is minimal or non-existent. OCD is a complex syndrome that affects cartilage and bones in joints. It is more common in young horses but may lead to the development of arthritis later in life. It is best to consult your veterinarian if you are considering a horse with this condition. Every horse is different as regards to long term prognosis.

Nerving is done when the coffin bone (third phalanx) has been broken. Trail riding is probably the best discipline for these animals. There is a list posted in the Racing Secretary's office of the horses who've had this procedure.

When you find a horse you like

You can make arrangements to have any horse vetted while at the track or even before you get there if you are in contact with the trainer or owner. Do this by asking the trainer for the names and phone numbers of the vet practices operating at that track. Be sure to ask the trainer who his vet is and choose one of the other practices to avoid conflict. There are vets at the track every day. Call them and see if they are willing to go over a horse if you find one. Veterinarians are at the track and happy to help in most cases because they want to see these horses find a happy retirement.

Cash is the best way to pay because the seller doesn't have to worry whether your check will clear. Cash also keeps you in a budget because you arrive with exactly what you're willing to pay. I know for myself this is important because I tend to fall in love with all horses. Many sellers will accept checks though, just ask.

When negotiating, bear in mind that trainers are interested in racehorses and winning races. If they are going to survive in this business, winning must be their priority. If a horse is not productive racing, they must replace it with another horse. Just like all other horse people, you have the trainers who dearly love their horses and the trainers who see them as a way to make a living. This makes a difference when negotiating. It matters to me and many of my trainer and owner friends where our horses are going. Be prepared to explain why you are a good home, if the trainer asks.

Keep in mind that age, sex, soundness and size all affect the price of a horse. Understand that racing people and show/pleasure people value horses differently. In racing a well-bred horse is very valuable, not just because of the breeding, but what the breeding means. In many cases, it seems that well-bred horses have class and carry themselves with confidence. If you find a well-bred horse who has been handled and cared for by good people, expect to pay more than for a horse without those attributes.

Stalls are assigned at the track and each trainer has a certain number of stalls. They are expected to make a certain number of starts per stall per month. Starts are races in which a trainer runs a horse. In Maryland, a trainer is expected to make one start per stall per month. It's not that easy to do when you consider some of the horses might be young horses that haven't started or a horse coming off a rest period and isn't fit enough to race yet. There is pressure to keep horses who are racing in each stall. If a trainer is not making his quota of starts for each horse, he risks losing his stall assignments. Resources are also limited. Most trainers do not want horses that are not viable taking their time or the time of their employees. It's hard to keep enough good employees for horses in training.

Trainers need horses that can race. They need owners to keep and buy new competitive horses. It's easier to get them to purchase a new horse when the retired horse is sold. Many trainers are happier if the horse is sold outside the racing industry. For me, it's because once I know the horse is not competitive, I do not want him to suffer the kind of life these horses usually have - dropping down in class to lesser and lesser tracks until they end up in a bad place. Many trainers do not want another trainer to get the horse and do well. Owners may get mad about this even if they weren't willing to do what it would have taken to get the horse competitive.

There are certain times that are better than others to shop at the track. Every track has separate "meets." These are designated time periods during which each trainer must apply for stalls and list his runners on the application. The end of the meet is a good time to buy. Some trainers are shipping out to other tracks and are selling any horses that are not competitive instead of shipping them to the new location. In areas that have a cold winter there is no grass racing, consequently the end of the fall meet is a great time to buy a horse that is competitive only on the grass. Unless a horse is racing for big money, it's not economically smart to carry him all winter until the spring meet. Grass horses tend to have less soundness issues and generally are raced less. During the winter, many trainers would like to have fewer horses to train because everything is harder to do during the winter months.

A great number of workers at the track are migrants. They all have to go home for two to four months each year. Their visas expire at the same time, causing a shortage of qualified workers. If you know when this happens in the state you are shopping in, it can be a great time to strike a deal on a new prospect. The foal certificate or papers as they are commonly referred to, enhance the value of the horse. Be sure to ask if the trainer will allow you to have them if you purchase the horse. Some trainers never allow the papers to go with the horse.

Up until 2017, each racehorse that has run has a tattoo on the underside of his top lip. It is a number preceded by a letter. This number is on the foal certificate. The first two numbers on the certificate are replaced by the letter. The letter denotes the age of the horse and repeats every 26 years. Lip tattoos often become hard to read with age. In 2017, Thoroughbred racehorses in America began to be microchipped and recorded with The Jockey Club.

Before you take them home

Try to get as much information as you can from the trainer/seller. You will need to know things like the dates and type of last vaccinations, deworming and dental. Find out what his diet/feeding program is. The amount and brand of grain and type of hay are important to know. Some horses are used to getting a mash once or twice a week. An abrupt end to this could be harmful. Most horses receive electrolytes so it's important you at least have salt readily available—which every horse should have access to anyway.

A note on registration papers: The protocol in racing is that whoever has the papers is the owner. We generally don't ever sign them because of the claiming process. When a horse is run in a claiming race, the papers are held in the Secretary's office. The money goes to the former owner's account and the registration papers are placed into the new owner's folder. No signing is ever done—at least not at any track I've raced at. A bill of sale or even a cancelled check can illustrate proof of ownership.

If you do not have your own trailer, it's easy to find someone located at the track to move your new horse. The nature of racing is that horses move around frequently, consequently there are lots of people willing to ship a horse for a fee. You only have to ask the seller for some suggestions of reputable shippers at the track.□

4 SO YOU GOT A HORSE OFF THE TRACK, WHAT NEXT?

When a racehorse leaves the track, he has no idea his purpose and destiny have changed. He still thinks he is a racehorse. It will take time and patience for him to become accustomed to this completely new life. Keep the transition simple. If he is overwhelmed with changes, he will become excited, confused, frustrated and scared.

Consider the type of facilities you have access to before making the decision of where to take your new horse from the track. I recommend keeping him stalled and gradually introducing him to turnout even if you plan to eventually transition him to full turn out with shelter. You will need a round pen or small paddock. He's been trained to run, so he's likely to run if you put him out in a large field. Horses can get seriously hurt when they run at liberty in the field. Especially when they are racehorse fit. The turnout area needs to be in a quiet place free of activity. It's also good to have a stall for him in a quiet area of the barn, but near at least one other horse. Racehorses are used to being around other horses 24/7. They are housed in barns with lots of other horses; they train on the track with lots of other horses and often ship on tractor trailers, with you guessed it, lots of other horses.

If you will not be taking him to your own farm, then you will need to find some sort of boarding arrangement. Use care when selecting a boarding or training barn. Be sure to educate yourself about how racehorses live and what they need. A major reason I wrote this book is to help with this. The barn must have solid horse management practices. It doesn't matter how fancy or pretty the facilities are or how likeable the people are. If they don't know how to manage the farm for the safety of the horses, you are in for headaches, heartaches, injuries and even the death of your horse. Busy boarding barns are doubly hard for letting down retired racehorses. There is a myriad of reasons, but one of the fundamental problems is the lack of a predictable environment. The caretakers may feed, turn out and bring the horses in at about the same time each day. However, each individual boarder has his own personal schedule, so people come and go at will, creating a chaotic environment from the newly retired racehorse's point of view. Although there are lots of people coming and going at the track, it is only open for training for a limited number of hours, making it necessary for all to adhere to a strict schedule. Most of the day at the track is extremely quiet and racehorses count on this. Even if you plan to eventually keep your horse at a large facility, I strongly suggest you begin with a small farm at first. Let him relax there and get the fundamentals of his new life established before moving to the bigger, busier barn.

If you're not comfortable with the prospect of transitioning a horse yourself, you can find a professional to do it. After the horse is let down, he will be relaxed and ready to start his new career. Nowadays there are trainers and farms that specialize in transitioning racehorses, and you may want to use one of those, but I strongly suggest you get references and check them out thoroughly. There are also farms that specialize in letting racehorses down for race owners and trainers. This service is needed for racehorses that need a break or have suffered an injury. This is a great option because they have experience in handling racehorses, which is what these horses are when they leave the track. They, however, will not begin the training process in most cases.

So the question is, how do you determine if a farm has the knowledge and practices to keep your horse safe? It's a complicated subject but I can offer you some guidelines. First of all, go and visit the farm you are considering more than once and at different times. How do the horses look? Do they come to the front of the stall when people come into the barn or hide in the back? Are they calm or excited? Do they have ample hay, water and bedding? Are the water buckets and troughs clean? Is there a good supply of feed and hay on the premises? Scrutinize the turn out situation. If horses are turned out together, do they have a lot of bite or kick marks on them? Horses are herd creatures and whenever possible they should be turned out together in small groups – with someone ensuring the groups get along. If there are too many horses trying to be the leader or there's an unjust bully, injuries are going to happen. Injuries almost always start out with a couple bite or kick marks and over time escalate to more serious injuries. One bite mark doesn't worry me too much because they could have been having a disagreement and this is one of the ways horses display their displeasure, but the second one puts me on guard and a third tells me there's a problem. Maybe it's your horse who is the bully but that doesn't mean he deserves to be injured.

The job of the staff or barn manager is to keep all horses safe. At my farm, as soon as I see more than one bite mark on a particular horse, I begin scrutinizing the situation. I don't like large herds; they are too difficult to manage. You will often see injuries happen with this sort of arrangement. If a group of horses, large or small, tend to run a lot, get ready for vet bills. I do not like to see horses do more than just a "happy gallop" at the beginning of turn out. If they run often, it's time to change the turn out arrangement – before the vet bills begin rolling in. Horses at Leighton Farm know that if they run, they come in. Period.

Some people feel that accidents happen to horses and that is just the way it is. If anything happens to a horse in my care it is on me, even if I did everything I could to avoid it. I have a responsibility to do the best I can to keep each and every horse safe and in good health. Yes, accidents do happen no matter how careful you are, but you have to do your best to avoid them. You shouldn't chalk them up to "that's the way horses are" and neither should the caretaker of your horse.

As stated earlier, at boarding barns, each person comes and goes at will and usually not at the same time every day. If their horse is turned out with yours and no others, and they bring their horse in from the field, your horse will most likely want in. Is the barn manager keeping watch for signs your horse wants in? If not, your horse will probably begin running because he's upset at being left alone or the fact that his only friend is gone. This is another sure path to injuries and anxiety in your horse. At Leighton Farm, we do not leave horses out alone. If they are in a round pen, there's a horse in the one next to him AND they are watched. If anyone goes out to get a horse to ride and there's only two, they bring the other horse in and put them both back out when they're finished riding.

If you do not have experience with transitioning a horse off the track, you need to get some guidance. Reading this book is a step in the right direction. I am available to answer your questions and guide you, but you should get a trainer to help you work with your horse and to show the both of you the way forward. This will avoid going down the wrong road. It's much easier to teach a horse a new skill than it is to fix a horse who has been confused, scared or frustrated. Unfortunately, I am fixing more and more horses as the popularity of retired racers grow. Interestingly, I am finding that often the "problem" horses are the more talented and athletic ones. I liken it to trying to learn to drive or work on a Ferrari sports car rather than a Chevy sedan.

When you bring your new horse from the track to the farm, he will need time to accept the new routine. Lots of horses will be nervous and unsure until they acclimate to this new schedule. Each horse is an individual and while most take only a few days to a week to settle in, some take much longer. One thing you can do to make the transition easier or to set the horse's mind at ease is stick to a very strict and consistent schedule of feeding, handling and turn out. You may not normally feed at exactly the same time each day, but you can always slowly transition back to your normal schedule of feeding "around the same time every day" once the horse has acclimated to farm life.

A horse that is newly retired from racing is "tight." This term means that he is conditioned to run both physically and mentally and is just that, tight. The muscles developed are those of a runner, not a gymnast, and consequently you need to be mindful that you are transforming this athlete both physically and mentally. In the first days after leaving the track the horse may appear what many describe as "waspy," meaning his abdomen is tight and tucked up. In the following days the horse will "let down" and his muscles will relax, and his abdomen will drop considerably. Along with the tight abdomen, there is a tight back. This too will begin to let go and relax without any help from you other than supplying some time. The time it takes to let down is directly connected with the mental state of the horse. Whether to give him a break while he lets down or begin some type of formal training is a decision that should be made for each individual horse.

A high strung and anxiety filled horse will take longer, perhaps several weeks to begin to let down. A relaxed type will do it in days. You can ride them before they let down but resist the temptation to force their head down if it is up. Allow them to let go in the back and the head will come down. If you try to force or coax it down you will generate anxiety, and the head will stay up even longer. In addition, you will start creating resistance because physically and mentally the horse is not ready.

Getting a Good Start

Racehorses undergo rigorous training and preparation during their early years. Typically, this training starts when they are one year old, starting with basic breaking in. Consider the implications if, despite years of dedicated training and effort, they find themselves in a world where they cannot fulfill the wishes of their caretakers. Only a small fraction of racehorses achieve success at any level. Although horses do not possess human cognition, they live in the moment with a heightened degree of awareness. They can sense failure, primarily through human reactions on which they depend. Horses have a sharp perception of their caretakers' emotions, whether it's satisfaction, disappointment, or frustration.

This is what many retired racehorses face. They are bred to be generous. Their heightened flight instinct makes them extremely sensitive. Most have deep, affectionate bonds with people because they have been surrounded by humans from a young age. Most are very attached to the attention and handling they receive. These horses leave racing knowing full well they have failed. As a result, many lack confidence in their work with humans. For all these reasons and more, there is a price to be paid when retired racehorses are rushed in their early training for a new career. For the most part, those who rush horses give little to no consideration to the horse's emotional and psychological needs. I see people bring horses straight from the track and begin jumping them or throwing new training principles at them immediately. This is done with little regard for the horse's needs, and once the lack of confidence displays itself as nervousness, defensiveness or lack of cooperation, the horse is many times blamed and punished.

Because retiring racehorses are so generous, they do their best to fulfill the ambitions of their new trainers. They will do things for them that they have not been prepared to do—they are after all, bred to be athletes. The lack of confidence will come back to haunt you if you move forward to the challenges of more advanced training or if the horse ends up with someone who is not capable of filling the great void with their riding skills. This is when the lack of confidence will rear its ugly head.

I am not against riding the horse when he comes from the track, in fact, if he is sound, I am for it. However, this is far different than jumping right into asking the horse to perform a completely new discipline without giving him the time to realize it is something he can do.

Whether or not you elect to have a pre-purchase/adoption exam at the track, I strongly suggest you have your vet come to the farm soon after your horse leaves the track. Your vet can do a wellness exam and help you make decisions such as whether to rest the horse or begin training so you have a baseline for that horse.

It is also important to evaluate the horse for the discipline he is best suited for. Simply because you like to jump doesn't mean the horse you just got from the track will be a good jumper. He may be best suited for dressage, endurance riding or something completely different. It takes time to determine what the horse will be best at, but the foundation he needs for most disciplines is the same. So, before you challenge the horse with jumping or showing, it is best to be sure he is thoroughly trained on the flat. He should be able to rebalance himself, stop and go without pulling on the reins and able to lift his back from leg pressure at the very least before moving on to the next phase. Ask yourself and be prepared for the possibility that this horse of your dreams isn't going to be the jumper you wanted. Have a plan for what you will do in that case.

When seeking a trainer for a retired Thoroughbred racehorse, I strongly suggest you select someone who has worked with Thoroughbreds. Do not get a Thoroughbred and put it with a trainer who specializes in another breed unless you are certain they have experience with – and the ability to understand and work with – the highly unique breed known as the Thoroughbred. Thoroughbreds are generous and intelligent. This can be a blessing or a curse depending on who is dealing with them. They are more sensitive physiologically – their nerves are closer to the surface of their skin. They are also more sensitive psychologically since they have been bred to run, which causes them to have a highly developed "flight" instinct which translates directly to reactiveness. Finding a trainer who understands Thoroughbreds can be challenging. You can use social media to ask for suggestions in your area, but don't stop there. Ask lots of questions and try to meet others that work or have worked with any potential trainer. Call the trainer to see if they will take time to talk with you and answer your questions. Go watch them work. A trainer must be good with horses but also must be someone you can work with and believe in. Once you find a trainer you like, don't be afraid to make a decision down the road to change trainers because it just isn't going well or because you and your horse have "outgrown" your trainer.

Based on some of the articles I've read about retiring racehorses, I am compelled to point out some things that I feel should be common sense but evidently are not for some people. For one, a retired racer has been on a farm in his past. Racehorses are not foaled at the track; they are born and raised on farms just like other horses. More often than not, they grow up with other youngsters playing and developing their athletic skills. Many enjoy rest periods or vacations during their careers while others are sent to the farm to recover from injuries. You can take comfort in the fact that your horse has been turned out with other horses during his life and knows what a water trough is.

Retraining begins as soon as you take your new horse out of the racing environment whether you ride him or not. You must introduce new rules. If you do not set down new boundaries, you are still teaching the horse how to behave, just not the desirable way to behave. You will not love your horse into submission, because that is not how horses operate. They need specific boundaries they can count on. This gives them security and trust in you.

The comfort of the racehorse is very important to race trainers and grooms. Therefore, your new partner is likely used to being cared for – A LOT. Uncomfortable racehorses are not happy and are more likely to injure themselves. For this reason, racehorses are used to being catered to. If it's hot, they have fans. Irritation from flies can damage feet and legs, so they are not tolerated; fly spray or nets are employed. Baths are given every day, weather permitting. Clean teats, sheaths and docks are required. Some people have expressed concerns about the confined lives racehorses lead because "they are meant to live outside." Though humans are descendants of the caveman, we live in houses with running water, heat and air conditioning for our comfort. Most of us have no desire to live in a cave. My point is, racehorses live inside a barn and are accustomed to being comfortable. Most are not going to understand or like it if you immediately put them out in a field to live. It is important to understand that it will take time for most ex-racers to adjust to their new lifestyle where they may not be catered to in the same way.

Your new horse may have a bad appetite. This can be due to the stress of the transition, stomach ulcers and/or bad teeth. Horses with bad teeth or ulcers may also be nervous, have a poor coat and/or dull temperament. Lots of retiring racehorses are body sore; this is not a permanent problem and can be treated with bute and more importantly, a rest period. An equine chiropractor or massage therapist can be very helpful.

I treat each new horse at my farm for ulcers and have their teeth and feet done. For safety, teeth should be checked before riding a new horse. I have my dentist come and do a dental exam as soon as possible, whether or not the horse had one recently. There are a lot of bad dentists out there and you want to be sure you and your new horse are starting out on the right hoof. Deworming is also a good idea once he settles into the new routine. Many people have a fecal done by their vet to determine a course of deworming. You should also have vaccinations and a Coggins done if needed. With regard to vaccinations, many horses at the track are not vaccinated for rabies since the horse resides in a protected environment.

Their Feet

Not all Thoroughbreds have bad feet. Many of them can have great feet but it's important to know that their feet are different than other breeds. They generally have thinner walls and soles, partly due to their breeding and partly due to the way they are managed and maintained for racing. If a Thoroughbred is intended for racing, they will get four shoes late in their first year or early in their second year and usually they will have four shoes for as long as their racing career lasts. By the time you get your horse off the track, he's likely had four shoes continuously for years. On top of that, racehorses are accustomed to perfect, manicured footing. These are the main reasons Thoroughbreds are notorious for their sensitive feet.

There is a transition period for the feet once the horse comes off the track. It's good to get a farrier who has experience with Thoroughbreds. He or she will know Thoroughbred feet and be equipped to make good decisions for healthy hooves. We've all heard it, but it's worth repeating "no hoof, no horse." Thoroughbred farriers normally use smaller nails because they realize Thoroughbred walls are thinner and even if the nail doesn't push through the wall quicking the horse, it puts pressure on the sensitive laminae of the inner hoof, causing pain or even bruising.

I encourage everyone to take any changes in shoeing slowly. Often people want to change the angles of the hooves which may well be the best thing for the horse but this must be done slowly and not within the first thirty days. When you consider pulling their shoes, think of the first time you go barefoot in the summer, it hurts! Then as the summer goes on, your feet toughen and you do great without those shoes. It is very similar for racehorses once their shoes are removed. I have seen people pull all four shoes immediately upon arrival to the farm and the horse almost always goes lame. If left unchecked this can create a vicious cycle of broken-up hoof walls, bruises, abscesses and lameness. This is painful for the horse.

If the horse is going to be in my retraining program, I have my farrier evaluate their feet and then we make a plan. It is subject to change if any issues develop. For this book, I asked Jamie Secoura, Journeyman farrier, what she would do with a horse off the track if she was free to make all the decisions with regard to hoof care. She responded with the following. "When a horse comes off the race track it is preferred to remove all 4 shoes for at least 2-3 shoeing cycles minimum to allow the hoof wall to grow out, harden, and expand. The horse's hooves will increase in size and the hoof wall will strengthen and thicken. If the horse does not tolerate being barefoot there are options to get them through the transition period such as using hoof boots, hoof casting material, and applying glue on shoes. On the track horses are shod in a specific way and style to optimize racing. This is not always beneficial to the health and quality of their hooves long term and when using Thoroughbreds for other types of disciplines."

I think it's a good idea to have the horse to go barefoot for the reasons Jamie stated but if I need to rehome the horse quickly, say within six months, I leave the shoes on because I need to be able to ride the horse and show him or her to prospective adopters. For the horses that enter my retraining program or horses whose feet make it necessary to address issues, I pull the shoes for a period of time. Usually from three to six months, sometimes longer. My general protocol for this is to leave their shoes on for the first thirty days to give their feet time to acclimate to farm footing which is not perfectly manicured like the racetrack. I then remove the hind shoes and see how they do. I expect to see some foot soreness for at least a few days, or even a few weeks. I don't pull the front shoes until the horse's hind feet are happy. Then I remove the front shoes and put boots on him. I keep the boots on while the horse is turned out for the first thirty days after the shoes were removed. After that I turn the horse out without the boots when the footing is soft, putting them on when the ground is hard. This requires more work for me, but the horse's feet will gradually toughen with time without the horse suffering. I want to avoid abscesses, bruises and the hoof walls breaking. Often with this method I can ride the horse in the arena after the first thirty days without the boots and he'll stay sound but this depends on the individual. Find a boot made for riding. They are designed to stay on when the horse walks, trots and canters. These days there are many boot choices out there. You just have to find the one that works for your horse.

Whether I pull the shoes or not, I stay very aware of how much moisture is getting to the horse's feet. I want to get the horses transitioned to as much turn out as possible once they arrive here but I want to avoid excessive moisture exposure to their feet. I normally put them out after the morning dew has dried and I sponge them rather than giving them full baths. Continuous wetting and drying of hooves often makes them brittle. Flies are another enemy of good feet. We use Shoofly leggins and good quality fly spray to ward off flies and keep the horses from repeatedly stomping which destroys hoof walls.

Feeding The Off-Track Thoroughbred

Don't underestimate the importance of a well-designed feeding program. Not only is it crucial for the horse's health, but it also contributes to their overall well-being. In fact, the type and amount of feed can even affect a horse's temperament, energy levels, ability to relax, and ability to learn.

Before I discuss my approach to feeding, it is important to note that many other factors affect a horse's well-being. These factors include the atmosphere in the barn, duration of turn-out time, and interactions with pasture mates. Some retired racehorses may miss the familiar routine of being in training, which can lead to restlessness and unease. It's also crucial to consider any potential veterinary issues that may contribute to perceived high energy, weight loss or anxiety, such as EPM, gastric issues, pain, and withdrawal from drugs. These conditions can make getting weight on the horse difficult, if not impossible, and at the same time cause behavior issues like anxiety and fear in the horse.

Developing a feeding program

I prioritize individualized feeding plans for each horse in my program because each horse is unique. From the beginning, I start with a simple, forage-heavy diet while closely monitoring and evaluating the horse with the help of my veterinarian. With the guidance of a nutritionist, I have developed general feeding practices that ensure optimal nutrition for the horse.

Finding a knowledgeable nutritionist is important. I recommend seeking one who is not affiliated with a specific brand to provide unbiased advice. Alternatively, you can consult the nutritionists affiliated with different brands to gather multiple perspectives and make an informed decision, usually at no cost. Designing a feeding program takes time and research, especially with the numerous feeding options available in today's market. I do my best to stay informed about new developments and products in real time. I then evaluate and update my program at least every five years.

Sticking to old habits or guessing is inefficient and potentially harmful to horses' health. With this approach it's unlikely you will provide them with what they truly need. A well-rounded feeding program supplemented with appropriate nutrients is essential for their overall well-being.

An often-overlooked resource is to read the feed bag! The bag contains essential information that can help you understand the nutritional requirements. For example, if the serving size is 1 pound and you are only feeding a half pound, you'll need to supplement to meet the horse's needs. Ration balancers can be a great solution in such cases.

When it comes to supplements, consulting with a nutritionist can save you both time and money. Educate yourself about any supplement you are considering and ensure it aligns with your feeding program. Although supplement companies may have their own nutritionists, it's important to remember their primary goal is to sell products. While supplements can be beneficial, overloading your horse can lead to unintended problems and financial strain. Always consider the base feed you are using and how the addition of supplements will affect the nutritional ratios.

One factor to consider with horses who have high energy levels or anxiety is calorie intake. Horses at the track are typically fed a high-calorie diet to support their growth, muscle development, and racing fitness. Incorporating a forage-based diet can be beneficial in managing calorie intake and promoting healthy weight maintenance.

Another factor is the percentage of non-structural carbohydrates (NSC) in the feed you provide. High levels of non-structural carbs can contribute to anxiety and reactivity in horses. I believe, from my own experience, that many Thoroughbreds are especially sensitive to high levels of NSC. From my research and advice of my nutritionist, I look for a feed that contains less than 17 percent NSC.

Weight loss and gain in retired racers

Weight gain in retired racers is a common concern that I am often asked about. The key to addressing this issue lies in identifying the underlying cause of the weight loss. It may be due to the breed's specific needs, stomach ulcers, stress or other veterinary issues. Stress, in particular, can cause rapid weight loss, regardless of how much you feed the horse.

Retiring racehorses experience stress, no matter how well they are handled. Racehorses are fed huge amounts of grain. Once a trainer decides to retire a horse, the horse receives less feed because he is no longer in race training. That, plus the horse's entire routine changing, can create stress in any horse. Keep in mind that even the most naturally calm horse, when racing fit, is a finely tuned performance athlete accustomed to a highly predictable lifestyle and environment.

For those reasons, I'm not overly concerned if a horse is a little underweight during the initial period after he arrives from the track.

Transitioning from the track to farm life also is stressful, even if it is an improvement. I use this time to evaluate the horse's condition, establish a connection, and give him the space to adjust to his new surroundings. It's important to provide him with a relaxing and peaceful environment where he can feel at ease.

Creating a calm atmosphere at my farm is a priority. Allowing the newcomers to observe and learn from the relaxed behaviors of the other horses helps them settle in more quickly. When trying to help your retired racer gain weight, it's important to consider whether they can relax, feel comfortable, and be happy in their new surroundings.

Gastric issues are a prominent focus in my feeding program, as research and my personal experience have shown that ulcers and gastric pain are common among racers and retired racers. Ulcers are found in most performance horses, which is why I provide my horses with 5 pounds of alfalfa each morning to act as a natural acid buffer. I want them to have the proper nutrition for training, and it doesn't hurt that they love it! Additionally, all my horses have access to orchard grass hay at all times, with hay in their stalls and round bales in the fields during winter. Forage forms the foundation of my feeding program.

It isn't only active stomach ulcers that cause problems for horses. Many times, I find that horses have trouble with processing (digesting) food efficiently due to the damage caused by ulcers. When ulcer lesions heal they leave scar tissue, not healthy stomach wall. If a horse has had ulcers in the past, his digestion may be impaired.

My first step is treating horses with U-Gard Solution by Corta Flx. It's basically the same as using Maalox for humans. It is calcium/magnesium but in a more palatable form for horses. I do not put it in their feed because I know from my own experience with stomach issues that the coating action of the Maalox is very helpful in reducing discomfort. To me, it follows that using it to treat horses with stomach issues will offer the same relief. I give each horse two ounces by dose syringe each morning before breakfast. You will find that after the first few days you only have to walk up to the stall with the dose syringe–most will come out and take to it like a baby bottle. It must taste really good because the horses here view it as a treat, not a treatment! This is a very cost-effective way to approach ulcers and, in my opinion, a good start. In more extreme cases, where the horse is demonstrating symptoms such as biting, a bad appetite or looking poorly, we treat with Gastrogard and then eventually transition to the U-Gard. This decision should be made with the help of a veterinarian.

Once I've addressed possible gastric issues, if the horse hasn't begun to gain weight and relax, I consider that Equine protozoal myeloencephalitis (EPM) may be the culprit. Unlike other conditions, EPM can strip a horse of its muscle development, making it incredibly difficult to put weight back on.

Diagnosing EPM can be challenging, especially in racehorses. Since they don't navigate small circles like horses being trained for other disciplines, symptoms may not be as obvious until the disease has progressed significantly. This often leads to retired horses being misjudged as simply becoming less competitive when, in reality, they have EPM.

Instead of waiting for obvious symptoms, which indicate advanced neurological damage, I keep a close eye for any potential signs of EPM. Indications of EPM can vary depending on where the organism is damaging the horse. That's one reason it's difficult to diagnose in the early stages when you want to treat it for the best outcome.

Testing for EPM is not conclusive; it only shows exposure, not whether it is the cause of the symptoms being presented. When I see three or more signs the horse may have EPM, I treat him. Normally, if they have it I see considerable improvement within two weeks of treatment. It's an approach that prevents unnecessary suffering and ensures the horses receive the care they need. If you suspect your horse might have EPM, it's important to consult with your vet to develop an action plan. Waiting to address the issue can lead to further damage. By tackling the problem head-on, you can help your horse regain its weight and overall well-being.

I firmly believe that attempting to rush weight gain can result in additional health issues. Rather than bombarding horses with various methods in attempts to speed up the process, I prefer to implement a methodical and balanced diet. This approach is designed to gradually and safely help the horses gain weight while maintaining their overall health.

To accomplish this, I rely on my experience, the expertise of my vet, and the valuable insights from a nutritionist. Together, we tailor a feeding program that suits the individual needs of each horse and ensures their well-being.

Some extra information about feeding

Sometimes you need to increase the amount of fat in the horse's diet to put weight on. We explored lots of different fat supplements and finally settled on soybean oil. While not perfect, it is 100% fat and a good source of antioxidants as well as being cost effective. A downside is handling oil can be a little work intensive. It can be messy, but its benefits far outweigh the disadvantages. If the horse hasn't been receiving a source of fat in his diet, it will take about 30 days for his body to begin to utilize it.

Horses that arrive in need of substantial weight gain can also be fed soaked beet pulp which does contain sugars, but in this case it is warranted because it is easy on the stomach and provides lots of fiber. Be mindful that unsweetened beet pulp contains 10-12% sugar.

Horses over the age of 15 that are in training or show signs of having had extensive stomach ulcers or are over the age of 17 years old are fed senior feed.

Now is as good a time as any to mention that a popular treat at the track is peppermints. You may find your former racehorse is a peppermint monster. (Sugar in this amount is probably safe as long as you don't act like a Pez Dispenser.)

It's very common for horses to drop weight during late fall and if you don't prepare, you will struggle to get it back all winter. To prevent this, you may need to increase feed and hay amounts to prepare for winter. Although we provide access to hay at all times, most horses will need more going into winter. Grass loses its nutritional value weeks before it dies, but lots of horses still prefer it which can lead to weight loss. As the temperatures fall, the need for hay rises. We begin to put hay in the fields around November in our part of the country (mid-Atlantic region). It's been my experience that simply increasing grain will not produce the desired results. Increasing the amount of hay maintains a healthy weight while the horse remains levelheaded.

Discover My Proven Feeding Program

If you're curious about what I feed my horses to achieve optimal results, don't hesitate to reach out. I'll gladly share my detailed feeding program with you. I chose not to include it in this book because I continuously strive to stay updated on the latest research and advancements in equine nutrition. By regularly evaluating and improving my program, I can effectively expand my knowledge and adapt to the latest research.

If you're interested, I can provide you with a comprehensive description of my feeding program, which I also share with my foster farms. Feel free to email me at kclark@goodhorse.org for a copy and review it at your convenience.

Turning them out

Hopefully you were able to ask the race trainer you got your horse from if he has spent any time on a farm recently. I believe in turning them out as soon as possible upon arrival at my farm and knowing when he was last turned out is a good indicator of how the horse will react. I like the horse to understand he is here to rest and relax, instead of creating anxiety by keeping him in while he worries about this new place he's come to. Let's face it, most horses are happy to be turned out and if they've arrived at such a place we should let them know as soon as possible. In the beginning, most do not want to be out long, but even ten minutes goes a long way to starting the process of letting down. The horse may take time to adjust to longer periods out of their stall because the stall means security and turn out may be too vast a freedom at the beginning.

It's important to understand that racehorses are trained to run, so you've got to be careful how you turn them out. It's a good idea to talk to your vet about using a mild tranquilizer when first turning a new horse out. This can keep the horse calm and avoid injuries as he transitions to turn out. If I feel the horse needs calming for turn-out, I start by giving acepromazine orally 40 to 50 minutes before the planned turn out. The acepromazine takes the edge off when given orally, without making them as uncoordinated as when given by injection. I believe in the "better safe than sorry" approach. Do not attempt to tranquilize the horse after he has been turned out and gotten excited. The horse may be difficult to catch, and the tranquilizer will be much less effective, if it works at all, because he is already excited. I wean them off of acepromazine within the first week.

Once the tranquilizer takes effect, I put them in a round pen, making sure there is a horse in the pen beside that's calm and won't encourage the new horse to run. When possible, the horse you put in the round pen beside him should be the horse you plan to turn him out with once he graduates to paddock turn out. That way they will already be familiar with each other. I do not believe in letting them sniff noses over the fence. To me, allowing horses to sniff noses with a fence between them is just begging for an injury. Their nature is to sniff, then squeal, then strike or kick. With a fence between them, they can hit their knees or even get a leg hung up in the fence. Not to mention the possibility they could injure you.

I turn the new horse out first in the morning when no other horses are out in other fields. If they do start running, it's not encouraged by horses in every other field on the farm. They stay out as long as they behave. Especially in the beginning, do not allow a lot of activity around the horse while turned out. Things like horses being ridden, tractors, lawn mowers and even cars driving in and out of the farm are all possible catalysts to get the horse running. The quieter you keep the atmosphere, the more likely the transition to turn out will be uneventful.

I do not leave the horse unattended. If he becomes agitated or boisterous, I bring him into the barn immediately. When horses pace back and forth along the fence, it means they want in, so we bring them in. I have found this works better than just allowing them to walk the fence for hours because a lot of time out while miserable will not help the horse relax. Ten happy minutes is on the right track for 15 happy minutes. Two miserable hours teaches the horse that turn out is no fun. After all, they learn what you teach them. Every horse is different, but generally in the first few days they do not spend more than an hour out; some as little as ten minutes. I gradually increase the time out and keep a close watch.

I know of more than one tragedy that occurred from leaving the newly retired racehorse turned out and not watching him. This is especially a problem if he is out with or around other horses and they are taken in and he is left out. In one case I know of, a horse became frantic and broke her leg and had to be euthanized. This didn't happen because she was a crazy Thoroughbred. It happened because she was a young horse who was used to being around other horses. Can they learn to be on their own? Of course, but this should be transitioned under supervision, not thrown at the horse all at once so he "learns to live with it."

When the horse is turned out in the round pen for two or three hours per day without incident, I make the transition to putting him in a field with another horse I know will be calm, preferably in a small size field with no trees or solid objects in it. I should note that some horses do not take well to the round pen and are fine once turned out in a field with other horses. The goal with the round pen is to allow the horse to settle into his new environment and adjust to being outside of a stall. You are looking for acceptance, not necessarily complete contentment, before transitioning to field turnout.

Since racehorses spend most of their time inside, they will be more sensitive to the elements. Most don't like to be hot and sweaty; they have a fan and get a bath when that happens at the track. Many are sensitive to the cold, too, because they are accustomed to wearing a blanket and being out of the wind and rain. Recently retired racehorses are much more likely to ask to come in than other horses, and you should bring them in before they become agitated and hurt themselves. You can gradually extend the amount of time they spend out. If they are standing by the gate away from the other horses, it's because they want in, not because of a lack of social skills. At the track, they are always around other horses—they may not be able to touch each other, but they are rarely ever alone.

If you're turning your new horse out on grass, make the transition slowly and carefully, as most racehorses have not had a lot of grass for quite a while. Grass is a good distraction, though, and can make it easier to get the horse to settle in. When you do turn them out, particularly in the beginning, you will want to protect their legs and feet. Protective boots and bell boots are good protection. I do not like polo bandages as they can come undone and harm the horse before you can catch him to fix them.

Developing the habit of coming to you when it's time to come in is important. It's best to call the horse and wait until he comes to you rather than going out in the field or round pen to get him. When he does come to you, reward him generously with pats or some other kind of positive attention.

Remember if you are uptight when handling your new horse, he will feel it and become uptight and nervous too. If this happens and you had a plan or goal, change the plan, don't move forward and risk a setback. Wait until he's calm. Whether you are riding, lunging or working on the ground with him, you will find he is better able to focus on what you are trying to accomplish when he is not anxious and afraid. I should explain that racehorses are not accustomed to being handled by anyone who is afraid or unsure of themselves. Horses are prey animals and their instincts tell them to resist and flee from a predator. If you approach the horse in that "nice horsey, I'm not going to hurt you" manner, he will likely interpret it as you creeping up on him. Everyone who approaches and works with horses while at the track has steady, purposeful hands and mannerisms. They are professionals and never work with or touch the horse in a tentative way. The race tracker approaches the racehorse with a purpose in mind and goes about the business of handling him. Their intention is clear to the horse and the horse takes comfort in that. This is not the same as manhandling the horse or pushing him around.

When to begin training for riding

I can make a solid argument for resting a horse before starting his "formal" training, but the training begins right away whether you intend it or not and even if you do not ride him. Each time you or anyone handles a horse, he is being trained.

You may decide not to begin riding or physical work right away. If the horse has any physical issues, it's best to provide a rest period before riding or lunging. There are many who mistakenly believe that lunging is easy on a horse because there is no rider, but in fact it is very strenuous and can be hard on the joints—especially if it is not implemented correctly. Any aches or pains will take care of themselves with a little vacation time. Some horses have been in constant work for a long time and just need a break. A rest period rests both mind and body, including the mouth. Once you do begin riding, you will be totally re-schooling communication with the horse's mouth. At the very least, since racehorses are fed much more than horses used in other disciplines, it's beneficial to get them off the "grain high" before riding them.

If you're going to let him down with a rest period, you need to decide on the length of time. Based on my experiences the length of time should be at least six weeks, but sometimes the horse tells me he needs more or, rarely, less than that. You should also know that bone heals in four months, so if there's a question or hint of a problem you may want to give him the four months. After that time, you can be assured that his mouth, soft tissue and bone structure are amply rested. For bone and soft tissue concerns, it's always advisable to consult a veterinarian before beginning riding or physical work such as lunging.

Your horse may seem depressed during the rest period. This may be because race training provides an adrenaline rush for the horse every day. There is an addiction to this, and horses can suffer from depression until returned to some type of training. Part of the letting down process involves breaking this cycle. Horses may also be depressed because they are not receiving the amount of human attention they got at the track. Someone rode them every day and the groom spent all morning with them. That amounts to hours of attention and human interaction. These horses need to keep working. They are not comfortable without a job and may be unhappy turned out without any sort of purpose. They might even produce unwanted behavior to fill the void left by not having a job. Walking the fence, weaving or chewing wood may not be old habits the seller failed to disclose. They may have developed because the horse needs something to do. For this reason, it may be wise to start some type of training schedule upon arrival to the farm. It may be very light and easy so as to rest the horse, but keep him happy, too.

Some believe that giving the horse six months or more off will "get the racehorse out of him" and then they can start over with the new training. This simply is not true. Horses do not forget their training. A lengthy rest will cause the horse to lose racing fitness and I suppose that will help in some way to launch the new training, but it will not erase what the horse knows. Trainers send racehorses to the farm to rest and then return to racing at all stages of their careers. Initially when the horse is returned to training, he will likely be lazy and go along with the program until his fitness begins to return. At that point whether he is a racehorse or retiree, he will want to do more—his competitive edge, if he had one, will begin to return. He will probably become more "up" when around other horses. I think this is one way that retired racers got the reputation for being difficult. In this case the problem is that no one ever told the horse he was anything but a racehorse. Even after a six-month break, he will still think he's a racehorse. The retraining has to occur so the horse will know how to direct his attention and athleticism whether you give him a long vacation or not.

Some people think that handlers at the track do not care about manners. Much of the pushiness experienced when handling a horse fresh off the track is due to the training to compete with and beat other horses to the wire. The race feeding and training program places the horse right at the edge mentally. That is taken into consideration by horsemen when the horse displays unbecoming behavior. They understand how good the horse is feeling and the stress he is under. Horsemen do not demand more than is necessary in the way of discipline. It is true that in many cases they let a horse "get away" with being rude. The racehorse is asked to be tolerant about so many things and race trackers are willing to accept behavior that may not be acceptable outside of racing. Confidence is a big factor and must be nurtured. Pushiness is many times a result of this confidence. That is not to say racehorses can't be confident and mannerly; it's just that when they are tiring and running down to the wire, the toughest horse, the one that wants it the most, is going to win, and more often than not he's the pushy one.

Some things you should know from the start

There are some issues you may need to address in horses that come off the track. Biting or snapping at you when you walk by the stall is more often than not an attempt to get attention. Biting when the girth is tightened is a result of procedures at the track. Lots of newly retired racehorses don't stand still when on cross ties or being groomed and worked on. They also have a habit of dragging you around rather than politely walking beside you.

Vicious biters are very rare and must be punished, but usually biting is just a way to get attention. Racehorses stand in the stall most of the day and night. They are trained to be aggressive, so some are going to pass the time by snapping at those who walk by. Keep in mind he's had a routine, possibly for years, where he snaps or bites, and a handler smacks, waves or even plays with him. It's his game and he gets attention every time he does it. If the horse is a biter because he is on Equipoise or some other hormone (these drugs are now banned from use in racing), in time it will be out of his system and the desire to bite will subside, but you will still have to let the horse know that this is now forbidden behavior.

If the horse you bring home displays this behavior, first try grabbing the halter and patting or scratching his head. This will change the interaction from confrontational to pleasing and you, the "leader," will remain in control. Over time, this will teach the horse to stop biting or snapping, especially if you acknowledge the horse when you are coming by before the behavior begins. The horse will stop looking for attention by biting and instead look to you for an enjoyable scratch. I want to stress that I am not suggesting you allow the horse to bite you. In some cases, you may have to take further action. I keep a short children's crop for cases where the horse just isn't getting the memo. I wait for the horse to try it and pop him on the end of the nose – not the face, not the eyes, just the nose between the nostrils. It normally only takes one or two times before simply showing him the crop changes his mind. You have to be consistent and fair when you take this route. This means every time, not most of the time, but it also means he has to display the behavior first and you must immediately use the crop. If you wait more than a few seconds, he will have no idea why you are correcting him and that is unfair.

A recently retired racehorse also may bite or snap at you when you tighten the girth. This is because exercise riders do not tighten the girth until they are on the horse and most of the time it is done while the horse is walking down the shed row. A horse newly off the track will resent the girth being pulled tight before you get on. He may snap at you in an attempt to tell you to cut it out. The best way to approach this is to put the girth on loosely and then gently bring it up a hole at a time over several minutes. This gives the horse a chance to adjust to it. With some horses you may have to resort to the child's crop, but the same rules apply.

Most racehorses have a large vocabulary of words because they are handled by humans 365 days a year while at the track, most of the time by more than one person. "Ho" is universal for stand, stop. I do not think I ever galloped a racehorse that did not know what "Ho" meant. Most learn the words walk, trot and canter while being broken. Spoken in a very calm way "Easy" means trust me, do not worry, it's okay, take it easy. "Over" is used when cleaning the stall while the horse is in it, and also while grooming or saddling the horse and the horse simply moves over! Ex-racers will remain on one side of the stall while I clean it and then when I quietly say "over" they move over to the other side. This is common at the track because stalls are done much of the time with the horse in it. A high-pitched whistle, the shsssst sound and clucking are all used to tell the horse to run and leave out of the gate. Keep this in mind when you are riding your horse or around others who are riding. Clucking and the other sounds mean GO! I often have to tell people who visit Leighton Farm that they need to lose the habit of clucking at the horse repeatedly. I don't know why they do it because there seems to be no consistency to their "clucks." I suppose eventually the horse is retrained to the point that clucking doesn't mean anything at all – he just accepts that some humans are "cluckers." Handlers at the track will ask the horse to pee with a soothing type of whistle, sort of like singing. This is taught to them so that the groom may encourage the horse to urinate after the race in the test barn. You cannot leave the detention barn, where horses go after a race, until they collect the urine for testing.

Cross Tying

Thoroughbred racehorses are never cross tied, but most will stand quietly on the tie chain located in the back of their stall. At the track, when outside of the stall, one person holds the horse and another works on him, for example when getting a bath. If you're dealing with a small trainer, the horse may ground tie or stand while one person bathes or works on him but that's not the norm.

Introduce the horse to the cross ties where there is little or no activity. Since they are used to being tied in the stall, a grooming stall is a great place to begin because there is a wall behind him and it's similar to his stall where he's used to being groomed on a tie chain. Introducing this new way of being tied in an open aisleway will make mishaps more likely. My advice is if you don't have a grooming stall, set up cross ties in a stall and begin the lesson there. Either way, understand that the horse is used to having a wall in front of him while being groomed and saddled. This is why I have someone stand in front of them when I introduce cross tying. Otherwise, the horse usually keeps trying to step forward.

I'll give you an overview of how I introduce cross tying. I begin by putting the horse in the grooming stall. I tie him with one cross tie while I leave the rope lead shank on, having an assistant hold it as she stands in front of the horse. The goal is for the horse to understand that this is simply a new place to be groomed and tacked up. I want the horse to enjoy and trust this place, so I normally give them a treat – not ten treats, just one. The horse must be required to stand in the exact same place I put him. If he moves even one hoof forward or back, I stop what I am doing and put his hoof back where it was as I say "Ho." This scenario will happen over and over until the horse learns I want him to stand until I ask him to move. I never lose my patience or get frustrated or angry. I simply correct any movement the horse makes by moving him back to the original position. I keep the sessions very short in the beginning to avoid going past his attention span. I gently groom him and maybe put the tack on. If everything goes well – and it usually does – on the second day I put both cross ties on and have an assistant stand in front of the horse. I keep the lead rope on the horse for the first week or so, draping it over his neck. After day two, I no longer need an assistant for most horses. It is inevitable that the horse will walk forward at least one time and his head will flip up. I want to prevent this the first few days until he understands and is comfortable with this new type of tying. Once the horse is comfortable and clearly understands cross tying, I start doing it in the aisleway. I choose a time when things are quiet to start this process. I repeat the same process of requiring the horse to stand in the same place I put him. I have had very few problems doing it this way and usually have the horse reliably cross tying in about a week to ten days. When introducing cross tying, be sure that the horse does not walk backwards or forwards to the point that the cross ties are taut. He is not familiar with being restricted in this way and is likely to pull back and break the ties and possibly injure himself.

Grooming

It's a good idea to gently go over any new horse with your hands to see if he has any sensitive areas, before pulling out the brushes. Thoroughbreds are thin skinned and sensitive. If they have ulcers, they may be resentful when you are grooming the girth/belly area. This is just a clue, so make note of it and use it in conjunction with other clues to care for your horse. Pay attention to the horse's reactions to your hands on him. If he has a sensitive area, he may kick out or move and step on you.

Racehorses are used to being groomed each day and having all four feet picked from the left side. Should you go around to the right side, they will be thinking, "She's doing it wrong," the first few times. They have, however, had their feet worked on from the right side by the farrier, so most don't have an adverse reaction and adjust quickly.

You should have little problem with bandaging and leg work. Racehorses are used to having their legs worked on every day. At a minimum, most are done up in standing bandages after training each morning. Most have been hosed, iced, and received rubdowns and therapies. Trainers have specific leg preps related to the actual race day such as a poultice or a sweat. It is common to train and race horses in protective bandages.

Racehorses normally get a bath every day the weather permits. For the most part they enjoy it. They are, however, accustomed to having one person hold them and another give the bath. This may cause the horse to be confused the first few times you give him a bath by yourself. A bit of patience to allow him to figure out it's just a one-man bath will answer any question the horse may have. It will also help if you've been working on "Ho" while on the cross ties to teach him "Ho" means stand quietly.

Leading

As stated earlier in the book, horses at the track are walked and handled outside of their stalls with the chain over their nose. When they are being walked, many of them bow their necks as they tow the walker around. People at the track allow this because this is a sign of confidence and leadership. Now this same horse is on the farm and this behavior is no longer acceptable. It should be stopped immediately to help the horse understand his new set of boundaries. You will find the horses don't pay much attention to you, the handler, in the beginning. They think your job is to stay out of their way! Walking politely has never been a requirement for most of them. If you observe them as you lead them, they are focused on the outside environment. To transition this behavior, I begin behavior modification, which is outlined later in this book. The first thing you need to do is get them to pay attention to you and this technique accomplishes just that. You can begin to implement it the first time you lead them anywhere. It doesn't do any good to say "Ho" if he's focused on other things unless you have a way to get his attention on you. Begin by leading the horse with the chain over his nose. Most horses will have more respect if the chain is there, even if you do not use it. Remember, it's what they are used to. With the behavior modification approach, it should only take a couple days before the horse stops pulling you around – if you are consistent about it. You cannot allow the horse to tow you at times and then tell him it's wrong at other times. He will never figure out what you want unless you are consistent in your handling.

Shipping

Racehorses are usually good shippers but many of them have only ridden in a van or large horse trailer. You will rarely see a tag along (bumper pull) trailer in racing. It is important to know this because it can be difficult to load a horse bound for his new home when his new owner arrives with a tag along. If the horse hesitates to go on, it is likely he has never seen one. They are much smaller than the vans and goosenecks he is accustomed to. Patience will get him on. It's new so you've got to give him time to understand it. This is one reason some people think the horse they have obtained is not a good shipper. He may in fact be a great shipper on a roomy rig, but afraid of the smaller space, especially if he has been rushed and forced onto it. Time and some firm patience will allow the horse to become comfortable with it. When you first start taking your horse places, remember that shipping is a normal part of racing. Horses are shipped to be broken, shipped to the racetrack and often they ship on race day. It's quite easy to transition this to shipping to school the horse or a show. Just keep in mind the horse will need a few trips to change his expectations. Racing is regimented and the horse has learned shipping usually means excitement.

It's a great idea to school the horse before going to a show or activity you intend to participate in by planning a few short, easy trips. I usually get them off the farm the first few times by taking them to a friend's nearby farm. I take them off the trailer, graze them and stick them in a stall while I work with other horses. Shipping training can begin before you even ride them. I suggest you complete the behavior modification before tackling the trailer training, or retraining, since it will help you keep the horse calm and in control. Once the horse is comfortable, you can ship him to a show you are not entered in or go to a park where he can be ridden with his pony buddy or calm companion. This is a very relaxing and productive way to introduce him to this new purpose for traveling. That's the real goal here, to create circumstances where shipping is relaxing. This may take some time for some horses, but if you do it, you will never regret it.

If you have entered in a clinic or other planned activity, arrive early and give the horse a chance to settle in. Most horses do well with a hand walk around the place to see it and adjust to the new environment. Lunging may help if you've trained him to do it ahead of time, but whatever you do, do not lunge him if he doesn't know how to do it properly. That will ramp him up, not calm him down. Always remember how taxing lunging is both physically and mentally for the horse. Don't use it to tire him and then expect to ride in a clinic for two hours.

It is unusual, but sometimes you will find a horse from the track that is a bad shipper. This can be caused by the horse not wanting to be a racehorse and can be resolved when he realizes you are not taking him to the races, provided he doesn't mind the new activity. Patience and encouragement coupled with many easy, short trips that are positive will usually take care of the horse's apprehension.

For more information, see "Shipping off the Farm" in Chapter 5.

About Running Off

What is running off? At a certain point in time during the gallop, the horse takes over and ceases responding to the rider's wishes. Most of the time he increases his speed drastically, but not always. I once had a horse go three miles at a very normal pace, she just was not responding to my aids to pull up. The outrider wasn't even aware I was being run off with until the third mile. No one at the track gallops a horse three miles intentionally. I found this more unpleasant than when the horse takes off and goes fast for a bit because I knew it was going to take a very long time for her to get tired. The outrider came out and pulled us up.

It may surprise you to know that very few racehorses ever run off. Not even once. There are horses who are run offs, but this is a rare occurrence. When the horse runs off, he grabs the bit preventing the rider from using it. It's never good to fight the horse when he commits to run off. This exhausts the rider so he doesn't have the strength to pull up when the horse becomes receptive again.

Most experienced exercise riders will tell you to try to hold the horse until the moment comes when he runs off because he may come back to you. The rider can often avoid being run off with just by sitting there and waiting. Often, the horse will come back on the rider's aids if the rider doesn't react and stays the same. Remember the horse is considering running off until he does it and fighting him will make him decide to go. But once the horse takes over, exercise riders relax and save strength for the spot on the track where the horse normally pulls up.

The most common reason a horse runs off at the track is the rider breaks the hold. Racehorses expect the rider to put their hands down and allow them to take hold of the bit. After that the rider is expected to remain still and maintain a consistent hold. If the horse is tough, it can be quite fatiguing to the rider. If the rider breaks the hold by changing the position of his hands, that's when the horse will run off.

Running off is less likely on the farm because racehorses generally do not expect to race, train or gallop unless they see a racetrack. Consequently, when you get on your OTTB at your farm he most likely is not thinking of galloping. The one exception is when you first introduce the canter, as explained later in this book.

It's important to remember we do jog and walk the horses on the track. In addition, we walk around the backstretch and in the barns. Racehorses are very controllable and are used to working in all three gaits. Once off the track they shouldn't be receiving anything near the quantity of grain they got at the track so they shouldn't be nearly as high. In addition, they will never be as fit. All this reduces the chance the horse will ever feel like running off.

If your horse is strong, a harsher bit is not the answer. Making a horse uncomfortable with the bit could actually get you run off with. Bits do not hold horses, good riding does. The more a rider worries about being run off with the more likely it will happen.

Say the worst happens and you find yourself being run off with. Remain calm, do not panic. Tell people in a loud voice that you are out of control so they can get out of the way. Do not fight the horse. Do not aim the horse at anything solid to stop him; this is dangerous and could injure both rider and horse. Keep your hands down. As hard as it may be to do, don't brace yourself against the horse or tense up. Soften your shoulders and go with the motion of the horse—that is how we pull up (stop in layman's terms). That is not the same as throwing the reins away or collapsing your body forward. If you brace against any horse, they will brace against you. Remember the horse will get tired and stop on his own. Horses rarely run into anything on their own. Obviously, schooling the horse in an enclosed area helps to prevent that option for the most part, but eventually you will probably want to explore larger areas.

The racehorse expects the rider's hands to be down on the withers most of the time. That is the "home" position. Putting your hands down on his withers can provide comfort to an anxious horse, but it may also lead the horse to think you are asking him to take hold. It's easy to differentiate. Just listen to what the horse says when you put your hands on his withers. Does he relax or begin to activate? When they take hold, they are not thinking of running off, they are simply taking hold. Some pull harder than others which is their individual hold. The problem comes when the rider pulls back after the horse takes hold. The dialog in the horse's brain goes something like this: "I've taken hold and now they're pulling, they're telling me to run." Then maybe you get upset and start pulling harder. "Okay, they want me to run faster." If you get upset about it, the horse will likely mirror your reaction, which likely never happened before because at the track his reaction is normal. In short, don't pull against a horse that has taken hold, you are telling him to run.

If you find your horse is heavy on the bit, try lifting your hands for a moment. Do not pull back, just lift them. It may seem counter intuitive but use more leg in order to activate the hindquarters. This is one reason why basic flat work/dressage training can be so useful. You can work the horse on a circle and develop the aids before going cross country even if it's just for a trail ride. This is true both for English or Western riders. Racehorses are on the forehand, that's much of the reason so many of them are heavy on the reins. You remedy this by building the strength in them so they can get off by using their back and rear end to carry the rider. It doesn't take long to get the basics on a horse. I can usually get an ex-racer to come off the forehand in our first riding session, for a moment or two. The suppling exercises discussed in this book will also help tremendously.

5 MY TRAINING PROGRAM

Introduction

In the following pages I will do my best to explain how I retrain retired racehorses. There are some basic qualities and tenets I bring to my training that are helpful. I am very careful not to ask horses I am training to do things they are not prepared to do because I know it will erode their confidence. It is my goal for them to feel successful at the end of each training session. I don't have a timeline with goals written in stone, but I have an order of accomplishments and I allow each individual horse to dictate the pace of achieving them. Relaxation is my priority with each horse because I understand that without it the horse will be difficult to train and ride. For me the lack of relaxation is a sign something is wrong.

I keep my training sessions short because the newly retired racehorse has a very short attention span. My goal is to make progress in small increments rather than huge leaps. I have found this approach more productive and even faster than trying to make huge leaps. Small goals produce small mistakes when they go wrong. Huge leaps produce huge problems when they go wrong, and big problems require far more time to correct and make up for, if I ever can. I do everything I can to make each day a success. I begin the formal training sessions with behavior modification. I encourage you to use these exercises too. It's an uncomplicated way to provide the basic skills your horse will need for his new life after racing while building his confidence in the new "system."

Not long after a horse arrives, I set aside a short amount of time when I work on establishing manners and boundaries. We work on cross tying, grooming, and picking the feet. I may even start the walk/halts with voice commands I use in the behavior modification, even if I don't plan to ride the horse yet. It establishes great leading skills. Through all of this, the horse learns to expect a time of day when a human works with him just as he did in his former life as a racehorse. This is the start of establishing our training space within my day.

Some general concepts

Every horse is an individual, so I cannot give you a cookie cutter program on how to retrain your off-track Thoroughbred. Whether you got him directly off the track or from a farm, each horse has his own training requirements. These requirements are based on variables including physical strength, conformation and temperament. Add to that previous injuries and different race training styles, and it's clear you will have to use your own judgment when working with your new horse.

I can say that with all my work with horses I have learned that time is one of the most meaningful and lasting gifts you can give to a horse. The time to grow. The time to develop physically and mentally. The time to figure it out. Training should go at the pace the horse is comfortable with. If the horse isn't doing well, slow down his world. Give him time.

It's important to establish a predictable routine so you can build trust and confidence with your horse. By starting with behavior modification and lunging, I earn trust and build a solid foundation for success because what we are doing is simple and predictable. We take it slow, allowing the horse to ease into the routine and gain confidence in our work together as our partnership is created. These initial sessions create a safe and dedicated training time for the horse, free from anxiety or excitement. Every step we take is carefully measured to ensure success, no matter how small. We avoid unnecessary setbacks by avoiding leaps that are too big to handle.

Although this phase doesn't require extensive time, typically just one to two weeks, it lays a solid foundation that we can always revert back to. It becomes a valuable tool when introducing new challenges, such as trips off the farm or problematic behaviors like issues loading on a trailer. By utilizing the walk halts and lunging exercises, we can redirect the horse's focus and regain control. Whether at a show or facing a trailering issue, simply recall the familiar walk halts to regain order.

Later, in situations where the horse is distracted or uncooperative,

I rely on the walk halts and lunging techniques to regain focus and control. By practicing these commands in a controlled environment, we can prevent issues before they arise, ensuring a smooth and enjoyable experience at shows or new locations. The horse already knows the answer—walk halts.

Newly retired racehorses have a short attention span. Their training sessions at the track, including a bath and walking to cool out, last at most an hour, and the horse isn't required to keep his focus on the handler and rider throughout that period. Starting them as I describe will allow them to build a longer attention span. Keep in mind the horse may become fidgety or even unreceptive after what seems like a short amount of time. Make note of the amount of time he can offer you. Just as with small children, attention spans are developed. In their own habitat, horses only need momentary attention spans. Pushing too far past a horse's ability to focus on what you are asking will result in undesirable behavior. You should always end each training session and interaction with the horse on a good note, rewarding them often for any attempts to do as you are asking. If the horse does what I'm asking him to do once or twice, I reward and move on to something else or stop for the day. There's always tomorrow to do it again. Resist the urge to keep asking over and over if you are not getting "there." Do something else and come back to it after he's had a success doing something else or quit for the day and come back with a new plan tomorrow. Less is usually more. You will remain in control of the session by changing the subject. He gains control of the session when he refuses, rebels, or shuts down. A pat or good boy is good praise. If at any time you and the horse suffer a setback, go back a few steps to what he was doing confidently and begin again.

On average, it takes several years of focused training to prepare a horse for racing. This systematic and rigorous training process doesn't guarantee success, as not all horses possess the innate talent required for racing. It's crucial to remember that these animals don't choose this lifestyle.

Your horse's self-confidence may impact his early training. The way horses are treated at the track can significantly affect their self-esteem. Top-performing horses are usually treated better; at the very least their caretakers are happier. This differential treatment can lead to a disparity in the horse's confidence levels. Many horses that don't succeed in racing often retire with low self-confidence.

Thoroughbreds are known for their generosity and heightened flight instinct, which often makes them exceptionally sensitive. From an early age, they are accustomed to human interaction and become deeply attached to the attention and handling they receive. This bond can make transitioning out of racing challenging for them, especially if they lack confidence.

When retired racehorses struggle to adapt to new training methods, it's often because they've learned they can't meet human expectations. In such cases, it may be necessary to invest additional time and effort into rebuilding their confidence and reassuring them of their capabilities. Ultimately, the goal is to help them understand that they can achieve what is asked of them.

Time and again I see people get a horse off the track and then in two weeks be proud the horse is jumping fences. In a month they have him at a show. That person hasn't spent any time training the horse. That person is taking advantage of what the horse already knows and the extreme generosity of the Thoroughbred breed. The question is, should the horse be doing these things at all? Has he had the preparation that builds confidence to be successful at this new endeavor, or is he being pushed and pressured into doing something he has not been given the tools to do? Does he have the physical development for this new task? Building a foundation takes time and there are no short cuts. The shortcuts you take now will have repercussions in the future. Developing the horse physically to move in a completely new way takes time. The best way to achieve success is through giving the horse time to develop both physically and mentally. It is not the good trainer who rushes the horse into a new discipline, it is the foolhardy one who wishes to show off, or the ignorant one who does not know that most "crazy Thoroughbreds" have been created by someone just like them. In many instances, because of his generosity, the horse handles the pressure for a period of time, but eventually breaks down physically, mentally or both. Please consider the welfare of the horse when you make decisions on how to develop and retrain him. Think of his future and ask yourself, "Am I giving him the tools he needs to be successful or am I just taking all I can from this animal?" If you are a taker, you will eventually drain the horse of his potential.

While working with Thoroughbreds, it's important to know that they have a very high sense of fairness. To illustrate this point: If a horse were to bite you (my old horse, Willie) and you immediately smacked his muzzle saying "NO," his response would be, "okay, you're right, I shouldn't have done it." You have successfully conveyed your point. Think about how horses communicate displeasure with each other; they kick or bite or pin their ears immediately. If, however, you wait one minute and then punish him, that is unfair. A horse has less than five seconds in which to relate two occurrences, the more time between two events, the less likely the horse will relate them. This fact has been established by the neuroscientists who specialize in how the mind of a horse works. The brain of the horse functions very differently than the human brain. I encourage you to learn about it if you plan to train horses. If you punish the horse outside of the five seconds, he has no idea why you are punishing him and not only is this unfair, it creates the wrong kind of relationship between you and your horse. I don't know about you, but I don't like people who treat me unfairly.

The Importance of Relaxation

As horse owners and trainers, our role requires empathy, understanding, and an unwavering commitment to the physical and emotional health of our horses. The cornerstone of successful training and a horse's overall well-being is relaxation. Before we get too far into the training of retired racers, we need to consider the role relaxation plays. Relaxation is the foundation on which everything you do with the horse rests. You can't have good communication, flatwork or jumps without it. Facilitating and ensuring relaxation requires skill and a deep understanding of the horse's nature.

I am talking about relaxation a lot in this book because I learned I didn't talk enough about its role in training and its importance to success in the first edition of this book. As mentioned earlier, an important skill for a racehorse is the ability to relax, even during a race. Relaxation is a key component of conserving the horse's energy during a race. Everyone at the track, including trainers, grooms, exercise riders and jockeys work diligently to encourage and develop the ability of the racehorse to relax. This is done through a multitude of methods. Schedules of care at the track are reliable and predictable so the horse never has to worry when he will be fed, trained or cared for. Grooms are relaxed and methodical in their handling of their horses. Almost everyone at the track is quiet. They speak softly to each other and the horses. Exercise riders stay centered and leave the horse alone as much as possible. For the jockey, aside from relaxing his own body as much as possible, it's imperative to understand where the horse can best relax during a race. For instance, some horses relax better if they break from the gate and stay on the lead. Others relax better if they sit a few lengths off the lead and then make a run at the end. Still others like to break and then settle to the back of the field, making a run at the end. If the jockey can't get the horse to relax and settle in, they're going to have a hard time winning because the horse who relaxes the most usually has the most energy at the end of the race. Tension eats energy and relaxation preserves it.

I am often asked how to get a retired racer to relax. Too often people relate the anxiety the horse is having with the life the horse had as a racehorse. That is rarely the cause because, as I have explained, racehorses are encouraged to relax and most have that ability.

To address anxiety, we must first identify the cause. Transitioning retired racehorses into new lives presents a unique challenge. These horses are accustomed to the structured world of racing and the inherent demands it places on them. They often need time and patience to adapt to their new roles. It is our duty as equestrians to facilitate this transition with empathy and a deep understanding of the horse's prey animal instincts. While working with horses, we must always keep in mind that, being prey animals, horses are always on some level of alert. This consistently opposes relaxation.

The amount of relaxation exhibited by the horse serves as a reliable gauge to how our training is going. Whether the horse is relaxed or not provides us with valuable insights about the success and direction of our training program. If the horse cannot relax, there is something wrong and we must do something about it.

Many factors can affect your retired racer's ability to relax. I will discuss several of the most important. First, the environment must be conducive to relaxation. Horses are sensitive creatures, and their surroundings significantly influence their state of mind. A calm and predictable setting, with suitable stabling and routines, can help the horse feel secure and at ease. Relaxation must be addressed in every part of the horse's environment. The amount of turn out and location of the stall in the barn is of consequence. The amount of hay he gets and the length of time he is able to graze are all important factors making the horse feel safe and secure which enables him to relax.

Second, the pace of training must suit the individual horse. Each horse will differ in the time it takes for him to learn to relax in his new environment. What takes one horse a long time to accept may be accepted almost immediately by another. For that reason, it's best not to set a schedule of goals for your training because you may be tempted to rush the horse or push him beyond what he can handle on a given day. A patient approach with the attitude that it will take as long as it takes will net the best results. How the horse reacts will help you determine the pace of training. If he is reacting with tension or anxiety, we must slow down, breaking the concept into smaller steps until the horse is comfortable with the pace and can begin to relax while doing as we ask.

Third, the emotions and demeanor of the people around the horse must support his relaxation. There's a lot we can't control with horses but we can control how we act. Horses are remarkably perceptive, and they mirror our emotions. It is imperative that we remain relaxed and composed, as our own tension will show up in our horses. Relax your body and mind. If you or the horse are already tense when you begin to handle or train him, you are starting out at a serious disadvantage. Begin each training session with a lot of walking to warm up the horse's body and to help him relax.

Fourth, pain inhibits relaxation. When the horse is having difficulty relaxing during training, you must first rule out pain. Until you identify the problem, you must slow down progress or back up entirely to something the horse is comfortable with. This may divert a training session but you can come back with a new approach after pain is ruled out. Then you can ask yourself whether the horse understands your request or if he has been sufficiently prepared to do what you are asking.

Finally, a horse that is afraid cannot relax. Fear causes anxiety in horses. Fear affects learning ability, focus and motivation. Fear does not desensitize over time. It can be quickly attached to an activity and once it's attached, you'll be working around it forever. You must address fear before adding any new challenges to a horse's training. You may need to go back to basics, address the fear, and then move forward. Your goal should always be to never scare the horse. They never forget that which scares them. Never.

Relaxation, often underestimated in its importance, is the main indicator of the success or failure of your training. Prioritizing relaxation is the key to effective communication, improved performance, and the overall well-being of these extraordinary creatures.

Behavior Modification

When a racehorse arrives at a farm after retirement from racing, he has no idea he's no longer a racehorse. Racing is not only a job for him, it is his identity. At Leighton Farm, the first training method we employ with each horse is behavior modification. The term sounds complicated, but it is actually very easy to implement. It is a method that will start you and your new horse off on the right hoof. Being consistent is the key component. I tack the horse up for each session because this is the beginning and the foundation of formal training. You will build everything you do with the horse on top of this foundation, including your relationship with the horse.

Behavior modification teaches the horse to react to voice commands, but it is also an exercise in interacting with the human in a polite and obedient way. This exercise is the basis of your partnership and sets the tone for everything else you do with the horse. After all, if the horse doesn't know to immediately respond to the simple instructions of stop and go, he is not trained. This lesson also makes the horse's job much easier, instilling confidence in him. He quickly learns to understand that his only job is to listen to you, and you will take care of him. This allows the horse to begin to let go of his flight instinct, which has been enhanced in his race training. Much of the anxiety horses display is a direct result of being put in a position where they are responsible for their own welfare. You want your horse to understand that he doesn't have to be responsible for his own welfare, that you will take care of him. When your horse drops his head in a relaxed position, he has accepted you as being the one in charge, and he now knows he doesn't have to be as concerned about his environment. This acceptance soon turns into trust and then into confidence. This is the beginning of teamwork.

I keep the sessions as short as they need to be to fit the ability of the horse to pay attention to me. This work should initially be done in an indoor or along a fence to keep the horse straight. He must look straight ahead, not at you or any other thing, and his focus must be always on you. This is one of the goals of this exercise—requiring the horse to focus on you while you work together. It's the beginning of developing his attention span. This seems easy, but you will find that most of the time horses straight off the track are paying attention to everything but you. This work is the first step in gaining the horse's confidence in you. It requires him to focus and rely on you during training. Another important goal of this exercise is to teach him to respond to your voice commands only, not your mannerisms.

Put the lunge line through the bit and under the noseband. The noseband prevents the lunge line from drooping too low on the soft, sensitive part of the nose. Clip to the bit on the other side. Be sure the lunge line is not tight. There should be a "droop." I use a lead with a chain since all racehorses are familiar with them and since I'm new to the horse, I'm not sure whether I will need extra help controlling him. I cover the chain with Vetrap to soften its effect. You will also need a lunge or dressage whip. Be sure to pay close attention to the pictures because if you fail to put the lunge line on correctly, it can tighten when you tug and stay tight, rather than loosening again.

Position yourself at his shoulder and halt along a fence or a wall. Keep a loose hold on the lead. The horse must learn to walk in your tempo. If he leans into you, use your elbow or a tap of the whip to keep him out of your space. Use the same voice commands each time, say the horse's name, pause, say "and," pause again, then say the command in a low but certain tone. For example, "Willie . . . and . . . Ho." Say it slowly but firmly. You are not asking him to halt; you are commanding him to halt. Be sure to give the horse a chance to respond. If he does not, give the command again and tug. Another method of communicating to the horse that you want him to halt is to show him the handle of the whip by holding it up in front of his nose after you have given the halt command. Gently bump the end of his nose with the butt of the whip if he does not respond when shown the whip handle. I want to emphasize that you are not whipping the horse in the face or even hitting him on his nose. It's just a light bump, no more than that. Normally after a time or two, simply showing the end of the whip will elicit the correct response—if you are consistent about it. A horse must stop and stand when told to – period. This is for safety. Be sure to stay by his shoulder and not give him any clues like pulling on the shank or stopping yourself as you say the voice commands. He's got to obey the voice command itself and if he doesn't, then you tug or show him the whip end. You only stop after he halts. If he backs up, stay with him, right by his shoulder and repeat the command, perhaps touching him with the whip behind if he continues to back. You want to use the word "Ho" rather than "whoa" because "whoa" is not as sharp and clear. To walk again, stand by the horse's shoulder and use the voice command "(Horse's name) AND walk." Give the horse the opportunity to respond and if he doesn't, reach behind and tap him low on the hind quarters with the whip. If he juts or lunges ahead, then tug or bump his nose and say "Ho." Stay alert during this moment of rebellion as he may run into you as he rushes forward. If you are quick and alert, he won't try that again.

In all your work with the horse, you must be fair. Give the horse your command and then be certain you have given him the opportunity to respond. The greener (less experienced) he is, the more time he needs. You will begin to see in his eye when he understands the word you are saying. If he fails to respond, then and only then should you reprimand by the tug, bump on the nose or whip tap. If you are consistent, you will be surprised at how quickly the horse learns to respond solely to your voice commands.

***You can see me demonstrate and explain these methods by going to the Good Horse Blog at* https://goodhorse.org/category/goodhorse/

About Lunging

In this section, I provide an overview of lunging and its importance in my training program. For a detailed description of how I introduce lunging to a retired racehorse, please see the Appendix.

After two or three days of behavior modification I begin lunging the horse. I encourage you to do this, too. It introduces small (20 meter) circles to the horse without being encumbered by the rider. I keep the horse at the walk. There is the possibility your new horse already knows how to lunge, or at least thinks he does. There are a lot of people who break racehorses and include lunging as part of their breaking regimen. However, it probably was not done in the disciplined manner I describe.

Proper lunging provides the opportunity to build a relationship and set ground rules with your new horse before riding him as you continue to develop his attention span. The horse's focus must be on the rider or trainer for the duration of all handling, which was not required as a racehorse. Lunging also develops the muscle the racehorse doesn't yet have to lift his back and carry the rider while maintaining his balance. He must be shown the way to relax and stretch his back while lunging instead of running madly around a circle struggling to stay upright. Once your horse is experienced at lunging, you can do it for a few minutes before riding to address any behavior issues before climbing aboard. If he is distracted today, you can get his focus on you before you get on. If he is uptight, you can slow him on the lunge and get some relaxation going.

Lunging should never be done to punish or tire a horse out so you can ride him. This will sour the horse to the real benefits that come from working on the lunge. Correct lunging is not chasing the horse around with a whip. If you chase the horse with a whip, do not be surprised if the horse runs away from you when it's time to come in from the field, since in essence you've been teaching him to run from you. Horses are flight driven animals so if you chase them, they will almost always run away. Thoroughbreds also rarely calm down when being chased on the lunge – they instead ramp up and become higher and more stressed.

One should never lunge a horse in only one direction. It will overdevelop him on that side and is a sure-fire way to make your horse sore. Always keep in mind that lunging is hard work for your horse. It is stressful to his joints, and the smaller the circles the more stress exerted on a horse's joints. Going too fast and out of balance can cause soreness and injuries. Just as in riding, small circles are for horses who are in advanced stages of training. At some point, you may want to lunge a horse to assess lameness. Unless you are experienced in diagnosis, I suggest you do this under the supervision of a vet.

If you've never lunged a horse, it's better to learn with a horse that already knows how to do it. It takes time to correctly coordinate the lunge line, lunge whip and horse, simultaneously. Add to that a horse that doesn't understand what to do, and you have a potential safety issue. If at all possible, I suggest finding a friend who has a horse that knows how to lunge and ask them if you can learn with their horse. It's usually not too difficult to find someone who'll let you lunge their horse. Lunging doesn't have the reputation as being the most enjoyable activity you can do with your horse. However, if done correctly, it can be one of the most productive and even fun.

***You can see how I lunge horses by going to the Good Horse Blog at* https://goodhorse.org/category/goodhorse/

You are about to ride your retired racehorse

Before you ride your retired racehorse, I want to emphasize again the importance of relaxation. It is essential that you have the ability to relax your body while riding your horse. If you are not relaxed, your horse cannot relax. Racehorses have no experience with tense or frightened riders. Riders at the track learn very quickly that a tense body will not stay with the motion of the racehorse, so they keep their bodies relaxed no matter the circumstances. They also know that the tension in their body will make the horse under them tense. In fact, the more uptight the horse is, the more relaxed the rider must become. Often the rider's relaxation is enough to get the horse to relax. It is natural for a human to tense up when he feels threatened, but one can and should override it. When you are tight it makes the horse uncomfortable, and it restricts his movement. He reads your actions and becomes wary of danger because your body is telling him something is going to happen—something bad. He depends on the rider for direction; after all, that is what we have trained him to do. Keep your body relaxed, allowing it to move with the motion of the horse. Answer any tension in the horse's body with a message of relaxation from your body.

The retired racehorse's natural concern about his balance can also interfere with relaxation. When a racehorse comes off the track the momentum (speeding up) he has always used to find balance is suddenly unacceptable. Without the momentum to find balance, the horse must learn how to carry both himself and the rider in a new way. He must develop the tools to navigate small circles and corners. He must learn how to halt and slow down using his rear end instead of his head and neck. He doesn't know how to balance himself without speeding up, which can lead to all sorts of trouble, especially for the new-to-the-OTTB rider. Sometimes his hind shoes have been removed making it even harder to find traction. As a result, he feels vulnerable, which creates anxiety.

Lack of balance is why racehorses have a difficult time establishing rhythm in their gaits at the onset of retraining. They had a very nice rhythm at the gallop and jog at the track, but these are momentum-based gaits. Sometimes people mistake this lack of rhythm for lameness because the horse may move unevenly in his quest for balance.

Rushing the horse's training without leaving time for physical and mental development will create anxiety in the horse. If the horse hasn't been properly prepared, he will probably compensate as much as he can to please the trainer. However, this will create a shaky foundation that will become more precarious the further the horse progresses. Listen to the horse. If he is nervous or keyed up, back off, find the reason and fix it before moving forward with the training.

It's important to lay down a solid foundation, both physical and mental, for the horse. The topline of the retired racehorse must be developed while at the same time the trainer must be very sensitive to the horse's real concerns about balance. He's been on his forehand for his lifetime and now it's time to build up the back and hind end. Your retired racehorse will probably be stronger on one side. Usually it is the left side, because horses do most of their work galloping to the left, but not always as some track riders do not rise on the correct diagonal at the trot. They may always rise on the same diagonal. This can be a cause of overdevelopment or even soreness of one side of the horse, not necessarily the left side.

Take care not to ask too much, too soon. Remember your new horse doesn't yet have the muscles to carry you in a completely new way. It's best not to put a timetable on his progress. Each horse is an individual. When you hit an obstacle in your progress, try a new approach. Do not keep applying the same aid you already know doesn't work. If you've tried it three times without success, why would it work the fourth time?

I believe in each and every ride you must reward, reward, reward, but this means you must set the horse up for success in your training plan each day. This is not to say that he should be spoiled, but the horse must know when he is doing what you want, and you must be careful to ask him to do what you have prepared him to do.

Mounting and Dismounting

Mounting and dismounting are two of the most dangerous times when riding a horse so take it seriously and train the horse to stand quietly and patiently while you mount and dismount.

A racehorse is used to being pulled out of the stall by the groom who then gives the rider a leg up in the shed row. As the horse walks down the shed row, the rider tightens the girth, ties a knot in the reins and adjusts the stirrups. All of this takes place before the horse walks out of the barn. This is what the retired racer knows about being mounted by a rider.

I normally don't have someone to help me with mounting at the farm. While there are people there in the event something goes wrong, they are not horse handlers. To introduce the new method of mounting, I use one of those portable plastic mounting blocks. I have four round pen panels set up in a square with one of the panels angled so there is ample room to enter and exit. The mounting block is in the middle. I walk the horse through it for several days before I get on him, stopping, giving him a peppermint and then stepping up on the mounting block before the day I use it to get on him. On the day, I do not rush, I give the horse as much time as he needs to be comfortable. Mounting must not be a big deal. I walk the horse up to the block and step onto it as I have on the previous days. Since I've already done my behavior modification the horse knows exactly what HO means and immediately responds to it. I say HO and when he halts, I put my foot in the iron, repeating the word HO as I step into the iron. If he begins to move, I take my foot out and as he walks around the block I repeat HO until he halts again. I need to get this right because I want the horse to understand from the start that the procedure requires him to stand and not move until I tell him to. If he doesn't respond to my voice command to halt, I begin making him walk around the mounting block until he is begging me to let him stop. This normally doesn't take long, because it's a small circle around that mounting block. This method causes the horse to make the choice to halt. Once I have gotten on and softly settled into the saddle, I reach forward and give him a peppermint. It will only take a couple days before he's standing quietly when I get on, waiting for the peppermint. I can wean him off the mint in a week or so because in that period of time the horse becomes used to standing as I mount. This works with most horses, but occasionally, someone must hold the horse or stand in front of him for a time or two.

When the rider settles down onto the horse's back, he must take care to do so slowly and softly. The horse needs a chance to "take" your weight and seat. Resist the temptation to sit too quickly. Give the horse time to adjust to the addition of your weight on his back. Sitting quickly makes lots of horses become fidgety and antsy while you mount because it causes discomfort and even pain.

I don't care how long it takes to train the horse to stand quietly while being mounted because time spent now will make him a great horse to mount forever. Once I'm on, I want him to stand for a moment and then I tell him to walk off. He is not allowed to walk off until I ask him to—this is VERY IMPORTANT. If he does, I make him stand again, pause and then ask him to walk on. At this point, I do not expect him to have a long attention span, so I only want a moment at this point.

Most horses are easy to mount, but now and then I get one that has ants in his pants. He probably was a horse that was mounted on the fly at the track. Meaning, the rider got a leg up while the horse was moving. If the horse is nervous or difficult, I will begin the mounting process in the stall, doing it much like I have outlined previously.

Dismounting can be a challenge the first few times because exercise riders almost never dismount outside in the open. When the ride at the track concludes, the rider goes back to the barn and rides into the horse's stall where the groom or hotwalker wait with the halter and lead. The rider dismounts and takes the saddle off while the groom or hotwalker takes off the bridle and puts on the halter. At the end of a race, the jockey rides up to the hotwalker or groom and dismounts. Consequently, when you or I end our ride on the farm, it's a surprise to the horse when we dismount outside the barn. Many will get ancy as if to say, "What are you doing?" Often I am by myself without help on the ground so I rely on voice commands and peppermints again. I halt, say "HO," give him a peppermint which breaks the ice, and I gently dismount as the horse chews his peppermint. This works 99% of the time. I have had horses who are worried about this so I ride in to the barn and into the stall to dismount and schedule the next ride when someone can help me. They hold him or stand in front of him while I dismount for the first few days. I also have that trusty peppermint to give him once I dismount. It only takes a few days for the horse to wait patiently for his treat as I get off. I want to note here that I don't give horses treats that often. Normally, I give them one after the ride—whether it was a good or bad ride. I do, however, use treats as a training aid because it works. If I wish to change the subject or alleviate anxiety for horses, treats can be very effective. I do this because it's the most efficient way I have found and they like it.

The First Ride, and Early Training

Safety is paramount on every ride. I always wear gloves and a helmet. I also wear a safety vest on new horses. If it's fly season, I make sure I cover the horse thoroughly with fly spray. I have another person assist me if I can, but it's got to be someone who is relaxed and steady. A nervous or tentative person will not be helpful. I am better off without help if their presence will make the horse uptight. The goal of this first ride is for it to be an easy, relaxing experience for the horse. Horses tend to start the next session where you left off in the last session. If I give them a good ride today, they will be more likely to expect a positive experience when I next ride them. For now, I'm training them to believe working with me will be easy and relaxing. Formal retraining lessons with small increments of pressure will come later once we've established some trust.

I normally get on the horse once he is confirmed at the behavior modification and lunging at the walk. This usually takes less than two weeks. Lunge the horse on each side before your first ride but do not lunge him to get him tired. Lunge him to ensure he is focused on you and to give him a warmup. A properly trained horse will respond to the voice commands used for lunging while being ridden.

As I mount, I lower myself gently onto the horse's back, keeping my body relaxed. This is our introduction as horse and rider. I know the horse will be evaluating the kind of rider I am. They always do with new riders. Although the horse may not have any idea what he is supposed to do, he knows by my relaxed body that things are okay. It's just another day in the life of that horse, not an earth-shattering breakthrough. Always remember, every interaction with the horse is a lesson whether you intend it or not. Make it a good one.

Thoroughbreds are more sensitive than most other breeds. Subtle aids usually work best. If you are a tactful rider this is a blessing. You use much less effort to elicit the response you want from the Thoroughbred. If you are used to riding Quarter Horses or Warmbloods, you may need to "turn the volume down" on all of your communications when astride the average Thoroughbred. Most Thoroughbreds are very generous. It often feels to me like they are waiting for my next request. If you are a busy rider, they will try to execute the seventeen things your body is asking them to do even if you don't mean it.

I put a yoke or breast plate on the horse and keep my pinkie in it. You may be more comfortable using your index and/or middle finger. I do this so I don't accidentally hit the horse in the mouth if he makes a quick move. Horses hate it when you hit them in the mouth. I use a straight rubber bit such as a NATHE or a simple snaffle bit. At the track, most racehorses go in a simple D-bit so resist the temptation to over-bit them. On these initial rides, I primarily use the voice commands the horse has learned during the behavior modification and lunging to guide the horse. I want a loose rein or at most a light contact. I know their back will be tight and I don't worry if they are carrying their head a bit high. This will subside in the next few days as I ride on a long rein. I keep my lower back very supple so I don't block the relaxation of the horse's back muscles, which will prevent him from letting go in his topline.

Always remember the importance of relaxing your body. When you get on a new horse, you are introducing yourself. Sit as relaxed as possible, be formless as if you've been punched in the stomach. Remember to breathe, especially to exhale, and let your shoulders drop down toward your hips so you do not convey tension to the horse. Do not roll your shoulders forward because that will pitch you forward.

I do the first rides in the arena because I don't yet know how the horse is to ride. The horse has been doing the behavior modification and lunging in this area so it will be familiar to him. However, I'm on his back now, which will bring out his previously learned expectations for training. One of these is that racehorses are accustomed to training with lots of other horses around them. The horse I am on may well be wondering where everyone else is now that I'm on his back. Expectations will vary with each horse. I will be carefully listening to him about any concerns he has.

If your horse stops and is frozen, encourage him to go in any direction rather than where you intended. In other words, just get him going. Remain relaxed, ride quietly and diplomatically, and use voice commands such as "walk" and "good boy." Overriding him in this instance could produce bad results.

Avoid doing lots of transitions, too many circles or other training during this introductory ride. Retired racehorses do not possess the muscle development or training for doing flat work in an arena. Everything you do challenges the horse's balance in a new way, which can frustrate and even upset him if you do too much. Be mindful that you are already introducing a new way of riding to him. Also consider that the length of an Olympic Dressage arena is 200', which is about as wide as many racetracks. Imagine how small that seems to the newly retired racehorse.

Circles and other challenges can come later when he understands you are doing something other than race training. Gradually immerse the horse into this new program. I keep my first rides short, around 10 minutes or less. I limit the gaits to walk because if the horse can't walk and relax, that is what we need to work on. I don't do many 20-meter circles. I stick to the circumference of the arena, changing direction on the diagonal or across the middle. You can easily do too much the first day, but you can't do too little. This is the introduction to the new way of doing things. Make it easy for the horse so he doesn't decide right off the bat that this is too hard and not for him.

I continue the short rides in the arena until the horse is relaxed, before, during and after the ride. For most horses it takes three or four days but I've had a few that it took a month. If the horse is extremely nervous and I'm sure he's healthy physically, I shorten the rides but continue the same routine until he is able to relax. The duration of the ride isn't important. I let the horse tell me when he's ready for more. I don't want him to drag his anxiety with him as I expand and increase his training. When the horse is relaxed in the arena, I introduce hacking cross country. How I do this, and build up to power walking, is explained in the next section.

Once the horse has done 30 days of hacking cross country, he likely has the development to begin proper work in the arena. I don't work in the arena every day. I normally power walk around the farm most days and intersperse one to two days in the arena, either lunging and/or power walking, and never asking the horse to get into a frame.

I ride the horse in a ground covering, forward walk and begin to do lots of big circles, while keeping the same rhythm as on the straight lines. This develops the turning skills of the horse. At the walk, the horse can maintain his balance with a rider and develop the skills to navigate his new work area. I start on the rein that's easiest for the horse. That's usually, but not always, the left rein. One exception is when I ask for the canter later in his development, I begin with the lead he likes the least –usually the right. My reason for this is that I have learned they usually offer the left lead readily and if I do it first, they resist picking up the right lead even more when I ask.

If a forward walk is maintained, you will find the horse develops quite a bit of fitness. You can put your lower leg further back on the horse's barrel to get a better walk. Legs further back communicate with the hind end. This is cause and effect, not a trick. Be careful not to put your leg too far back though. Kicking, shoving, and pounding on the horse will make the horse uptight resulting in short and quick strides which is not what I want.

Once the horse is able to walk purposefully with some relaxation and suppleness, on circles and straight lines, I begin to add trot work. I start trot work on the lunge, but I keep these lunge lessons short. I don't like long lunge sessions for horses. I believe it's too hard on them. When you ride the trot, post, don't sit, because the horse's back can't support the sitting trot at this stage. I make sure to post low and softly because I don't want to drive the horse with my posting as riders do at the track. I want his back to remain loose and relaxed.

I don't do many trot circles initially. I save those for the lunge so the horse can find his balance without the aid of the rider. The amount of time I spend on each step varies from horse to horse. I

Outrider Kaymarie Kriedel ponys a horse as four baby horses gallop by.

would estimate on average we are doing 15 minutes of walk and 15 minutes of trot at the end of 30 days. The horse's ability to relax during the work tells me how much I can do. I then add a walking hack around the farm before the work in the arena, extending the time I ride the horse each day without drilling him. The hack will serve as our warm up.

Power walking

Physical development should begin by hacking cross country, and in particular power walking the horse over the naturally undulating ground found in the environment found outside of manicured arenas. There is nothing fancy or intriguing about power walking, but it's incredibly effective in introducing the new tools a racehorse will need to find balance. It's usually the one gait where the rider is telling the retired racehorse to go instead of Ho. Initially in the trot and canter gaits the rider is often saying Ho and go easy, so I find this a great place to begin.

When you go cross country or on the trail for the first time, it's a good idea to go with at least one other horse. The ex-racer is much more likely to relax if other horses are present. He may never have trained alone before since there are always other horses on the track. As mentioned earlier, we use horses known as ponies at the racetrack to lead or chaperone racehorses both in the morning and afternoon. They also catch loose horses. Racehorses that are schooled properly will run to the pony when they get loose. Almost every racehorse knows how to pony and finds comfort and confidence when they are beside the pony. Racehorses trust the pony and rely on their judgment.

You can use this to your advantage to help your retired racehorse relax in your early rides. If you walk with another horse, keeping your horse's head at the other horse's shoulder, this is the "ponying" spot. Most OTTBs will relax and find confidence while strolling along in that position. It helps if the company you've chosen is a calm and relaxed type, but he doesn't have to know how to pony a racehorse. The rider on the other horse can drop his hand down as if he's holding a lead strap. The sight of that hand will make the retired racehorse feel even more secure. They know the pony is a place of security and now you do, too.

Power walking can be done cross country or in the arena. It keeps the horse tuned in to the rider instead of what is happening around him. It also teaches him how to carry the rider using his back in a gait that is easiest for him to keep his balance. This work develops the topline of the horse without any pounding of his legs. It also develops the area most difficult to strengthen directly behind the saddle.

In the power walk, the horse's back is swinging, and he is stepping far and propelling himself forward from behind. For him to do this, your back must be very relaxed to allow his back to relax and move. You will have to encourage the horse to stay in a forward walk. Horses at liberty rarely power walk, they just break into the trot to get there faster. The horse should be asked to take bigger steps than he offers. This is achieved through putting your legs further back, which connects them with the horse's rear end, softening your lower back and when necessary, touching the horse behind your leg with the whip. It is important not to shove your seat at him or move around in the tack as this can produce a stiff and hurried walk. You are seeking a relaxed, rhythmic and ground-covering walk. This work begins to develop the topline making it possible for the horse to lift his back to carry the rider and to distribute his weight on all four corners/legs to find balance. Developing the horse physically in this way gives him the tools needed to be successful at this new way of carrying the rider. Rushing the horse into a new frame before he is ready will result in undesirable behavior because the horse has no choice but to fall on the forehand and rush. He doesn't have the muscle development for self-carriage. In many instances, the horses that are rushed end up being over bitted because they have been given no option but to lay on the bit. Laying on the bit is a sure sign of physical weakness. Once developed correctly, the horse will carry himself, lifting his front end with his back and hindquarters, but this development takes time. There are no short cuts to getting there.

When you first start riding cross country or out of a riding ring, expect your horse to have trouble negotiating uneven footing. Racetracks are harrowed at least once each morning during training hours, and they are harrowed and watered between each race. This means that retired racehorses need time to acclimate to the undulating ground found on many farms. They may stumble or look at the ground. This will pass quickly for most as they adjust to uneven ground. A recently retired racehorse may also tire easily when going up hills, so limit hill work until he builds strength and balance or he will become sore and sour.

Power walking teaches the horse to be forward in his new environment. Forward is good and is something every exercise rider and jockey knows. It is also the goal of every show and pleasure riding discipline I know of. When the racehorse is broke to ride, the answer to most any question or problem that arises is, "go forward." This creates a forward-thinking horse which is good for any discipline. It will come in handy while jumping that trappy fence or while working on those transitions from collection to extension and of course, while trying to walk by the scariest plastic bag in the world.

It's not unusual for me to spend a month power walking, alternating between the arena and cross country. During this time, I am developing the back and hind end muscles that are necessary to carry me in the trot and canter. If I have to put the horse up for adoption on the website right away, I still spend most of the time power walking and only do the walk, trot, and canter to produce a video for showing the horse to prospective owners.

Power walking may seem boring and unglamorous, but that is what many good training methods are. They lack excitement but build the confidence and good results that create a solid foundation for all future work.

Use of the Reins and Hands

When retraining, putting a harsh bit in the horse's mouth to stop him from taking hold of the bit is NOT recommended. Racehorses trust the bit and many times, the use of a severe bit will result in an out of control horse. If the horse cannot connect with the bit then he can't have the correct relationship with it either. In essence you are throwing the steering wheel out of the car. When the bit is more than the horse requires, he can become resentful or frightened and is more likely to run off to get away from the bit. Bits do not hold horses, good riding and training does. The proper approach is to put a snaffle or other mild bit in and re-school the mouth. Severe bits are torture to the horse and are a psychological crutch for inept riders. I can't stress enough that the mouth of the racehorse needs to be retrained, not abused into submission.

The reins are an accelerator, not only in racing, but with all horses! Racehorses run when the jockey or exercise rider pulls on the reins.

They are not taught to do this, it is the natural reaction of any horse to speed up when the reins are pulled. When a rider pulls on the reins, it changes the horse's balance, and his natural remedy is to go faster. Race riders capitalize on this reaction because it is more efficient to utilize the inborn reactions of horses than to teach them to react to something. In short, the horse doesn't have to think about speeding up when the reins are pulled, he simply reacts. You must remember that when you pull on the reins, you are asking the horse to go faster.

The primary use of the reins is as a straightening influence. Whenever you employ the reins, you must first employ the leg to the rein. Right leg to left rein and left leg to right rein equals a straight horse. Any bend in the horse's body must come from the leg. If you want to use a leading rein to turn the horse, open it, do not pull back.

The proper way to stop any riding horse is to sit up, close the legs and hands, riding his hind end to the front. Most racehorses are not strong enough to walk their rear end under nor have they ever been asked to do so. In order to do this, they have to tilt their pelvis and lift their back under the rider. The way to get there is to lift the hands up without pulling, until the horse stops. This discourages the horse from shifting his weight onto the forehand at the halt and helps to shift the center of gravity backward. Think of a seesaw: head up shifts weight to back, rear down. You must, however, be careful not to pull because this will cause the horse to "bonk" onto the forehand. Stick your elbows on your side to keep yourself honest. Lift your hands with your thumbs up until the horse stops. The first time or two you may have to lift until the horse flings his head up, but he will soon learn when you begin to lift to halt or slow down.

Racehorses are not laterally supple, that is, from side to side. The reason is that straight is faster. Think of throwing a spear through the air as opposed to a rope, which will go further and faster? Racehorses are usually very locked up or tight in the poll. This needs to be addressed because you cannot half halt or communicate with correct rein aids until the poll is unlocked. There are simple suppling exercises you can do from the ground and from the horse's back.

Suppling the Horse

There are lots of suppling exercises that help "unlock" your retired racehorse or any horse for that matter. Racehorses never bend their bodies, even around the sweeping turns of the racetrack. They are laterally straight because that is the most efficient way to go fast. Since they are trained and conditioned to gallop and race, they are never suppled either laterally or longitudinally. All disciplines other than racing require some degree of both types of suppleness. Dressage riders especially will understand this. Lateral is side to side and longitudinal is front to rear, meaning his head has come down because his back is up because he is stepping under behind.

Lateral suppling is something I do as soon as the horse is comfortable with his new situation. I may do the basic suppling exercise before I even begin work in the arena. It's not uncommon for me to do it the first day, but I decide this by his level of comfort with this new training. Most ex-racers are "locked" at the poll. Asking them to move their head from side to side is very difficult. Unlocking them is key to communication with the rider and self-carriage. It makes a better connection with the bit immediately. I do it every day with dressage horses and jumpers I've had for years. Neck suppling exercises help to break down the horse's defensiveness. This will in turn enable open communication with the horse without having to hold him with the reins. It's one of the steps that I use to encourage the horse to relax and become responsive to the rider in a positive way.

By suppling the neck, the rider is working toward getting the horse to drop his neck, to let go both physically and mentally. A horse cannot drop his head without giving himself to some extent to the rider unless some external device is being used. When the horse drops his head, he has to stretch his back to some extent. Once the back begins to stretch, the horse will begin to relax and direct his attention to the rider.

To keep the head down, the rider needs to take care not to pull on the reins since pulling on the reins triggers defensiveness in the horse and will cause him to pull back. Once the horse's head is down, the rider should only "catch" the head when it tries to swing up to keep the horse from escaping the bit. It is important to ride young horses or horses just beginning the training on a loose rein. Usually, it is best to keep your arms long but the reins short so you have the effect of a loose rein while maintaining the ability to react quickly to something untoward.

When a horse's back is retracted, as it is in early training, his brain is tense. He tends to be reactive to his environment because his posture is that of flight. The horse after all is primarily a physical animal and needs to be worked with as such. Even humans, the "reasoning" animal, can rarely be talked out of tension without some strategic physical activity. When the horse's muscles are tight, he is in a defensive mode and is alert to any danger, imagined or otherwise. It therefore becomes paramount to break down this defensiveness.

If the horse's poll is locked and the rider puts his legs on to halt or ask the horse to lift his back, the aids will not work until the horse lets go in his back. Suppling exercises help the horse unlock his poll.

The simplest suppling exercise I use is to put my hand on my knee and completely release the opposing rein. I am careful not to pull the horse's head in more than I can keep his forehead vertical. I put my hand on my knee so that when the horse gives in or submits, I do not take more, which would be unfair. With my hand on my knee when he submits there is instant reward (give). I then do the same process on the opposite rein. When you introduce this exercise, the horse may step in a small circle. Tell him Ho and wait for him to halt and give in. The circling helps the horse to unlock his body and become supple. If the horse begins to panic, release the hold, but that rarely happens; normally, the horse circles and finally gives in.

Once the horse gives in on both sides, hold – do not pull – the outside rein. Open the inside rein to activate the outside rein more, without bending the horse's neck to the inside, and ask the horse to walk on using more inside leg than outside leg. The horse will not want to do this because it is much easier to drag you along on the forehand with his front legs. By doing this, he will be required to step forward with his hind legs first. This is difficult so be patient. He may back up, stay relaxed and lean back if he does this. Keep asking and he will eventually take the step forward from behind. You must make a fuss about how good he is because this is very difficult for the retired racehorse to do.

I employ crest flopping in conjunction with this exercise. Have contact with both reins without pulling. Close one hand on the rein, soften and then close the other. This should instigate the flopping of the horse's crest which involves the entire topline of the horse, not just the crest of the neck which you can see. Horses LOVE this!

If I am riding a horse that just won't let go of the bit as I try to supple him, I will take his head back and forth very quickly, taking care to release the outside rein, to try to break down his resistance. Or I will put my hand under my knee (to block any chance of pulling) and hold it there until the horse gives in and stands quietly without pulling on the bit, again, making sure I release the outside rein. I use this same technique to walk forward if I cannot get the horse to step forward without using his head and neck.

Circles are suppling exercises. You begin by showing the horse how to navigate a 20-meter circle. Then you can spiral in and spiral out to get that inside hind more active. Quick changes of direction, especially when coupled with transitions into and out of the gait are time honored ways of getting the horse supple. I have found that I can get there more quickly when I incorporate the neck suppling, even if I only do the initial neck suppling to try to soften the horse's neck muscles before getting to the other suppling exercises. Until the rider can access the horse's haunches, he is limited to the extent to which he can control the horse: he must have access to the haunches to bring the back up. Until the horse's back is up, he will not be entirely receptive to the rider.

Turning

All racehorses steer by the rider putting weight in the inside stirrup. Show and riding horses turn from weight in the inside seat bone and stirrup. Both are reactions of the horse to the same aid. They do not need to be taught this. This is a reaction by the horse to a particular stimulus. This is the basis of classical horsemanship. The horse simply reacts to an aid rather than having to think about it or learn it. At the track, racehorses steer to change lanes, but they rarely actually turn. Turning in confined arenas and small areas is a new challenge. The ex-racehorse is going to need you to tell him how to do it.

Horses are worried about falling. Their natural way of keeping balance is to go faster. Small circles are the first exercise where the horse must find balance by distributing his weight on all four corners/legs. If you began his training on the lunge at the walk it's going to be much easier for him since by the time you get on him he will already have started to develop the fitness for self-carriage on circles. Introducing the rider into the equation is a bigger challenge.

The correct aid for turning is to put more weight on the inside seat bone and/or more weight into the inside stirrup and seat bone without leaning. Think of stepping into the inside stirrup or sitting more on the inside seat bone by lengthening the inside of your body. The proper use of the reins at this stage is to engage the outside rein and open or lead with the inside rein without bending the neck. Do not pull back on the inside rein. Pulling on the inside rein causes the horse to over-bend his neck to the inside and throw his outside shoulder sideways in an attempt to keep his balance. Once the horse is over bent it becomes impossible for him to go in the direction you want. He cannot turn while jackknifed because he's lost all balance and must shift his weight to stay upright. He'll follow his outside shoulder moving sideways – all the while wondering why you want to do this. You must realize he is doing exactly what you are asking him to do at that point.

To restore the balance, you straighten him with the outside rein—getting off the inside rein—and then attempt the turn again. When the horse is over bent or rubber necking and you pull more on the inside rein, he will be further over bent and move sideways faster. It can be helpful to carry a whip, holding it in the outside hand against the outside shoulder to help prevent the horse from throwing his shoulder out on the turn.

How do I know if the training is going well?

Whether you are doing it yourself or have the help of a trainer, how do you know if the training is going well? One strong indicator is the horse's anxiety level and or resistance. Yes, you guessed it, this is a lack of relaxation and as always, relaxation is our goal during all training sessions. Once the horse has settled into his new environment, he should be relaxed most of the time. If the horse is displaying anxiety or tension, it should be short-lived.

When a horse is over-challenged, doesn't understand, is in pain or just plain can't do something, he will almost always display his predicament in one of two ways: shut down/internalize or actively show anxiety. Most Thoroughbreds display their distress about training through anxiety. You know you are introducing or insisting on something too soon when you must force it and the horse responds with resistance. With resistance usually comes anxiety in the Thoroughbred.

You should always have a plan and goal for a training session, but it must be subject to change based on the way things are going that day. If the horse starts out with some anxiety or tension but it diminishes or even disappears during the training session, then you are on track. If, however, the anxiety increases, it's time to change the session plan for the day. Examine what happened and try a new approach. If you introduce things like jumping or leg-yielding, or any new concept, while your horse is upset, you will attach that anxiety to the activity. He will not reason, it just will be the reality you gave to him. It's up to you to make sure the horse learns to relax and that your goals are attainable for the horse each and every day.

As an example, I have seen considerable anxiety generated in horses when the rider is introducing and insisting on lead changes before the horse is ready. This causes the horse to develop anxiety associated with the changes. You know it's too soon when you must force the changes and the horse resists. If you begin the lead changes in the warmup and the horse develops anxiety and resistance and you plan to jump him after the warmup, he will carry that anxiety over to the jump session. The rider should be able to feel the anxiety building in the horse. I wouldn't move on until I extinguished the anxiety by identifying and dealing with the cause, even if it means not keeping to the plan that day. This is just one example of how to identify whether the training is going well. To sum it up – listen to your horse.

Canter Work

Once the horse is comfortable with circles at the trot in the arena, I begin canter work. The reason I wait on the canter is because this gait challenges the balance of the horse the most. One phase of the canter stride has all four feet off the ground. I introduce canter on the lunge. The horse is usually a bit apprehensive initially which is fine with me. I don't want him to run into the canter because this will put him out of balance from the first canter stride. It's hard and I may have to live with a few quick steps at first, but my goal is for the horse to strike into the canter from the trot as soon as he possibly can. Keeping the duration of the canter short will alleviate the lack of balance the horse experiences. I do not allow the horse to race around me in the canter looking for balance. Instead, I show him the way to balance with a downward transition to the trot after two or three steps. Motorcycling around a circle can hurt them and will generate anxiety. The transitions in and out of the canter build the strength needed to produce a quality, balanced canter. Keeping the canter to a half circle at most during the initial stage will enable the horse to quickly learn he can regain his balance by breaking to the trot. The horse will stop worrying about being out of balance because we are not allowing him to canter far before we correct the loss of balance with a transition. This will someday translate to a half halt within the canter to regain balance.

I use the voice command for canter when I begin canter work while riding the horse. Since I won't ask for the canter while riding the horse until he can strike into the canter on the lunge without any quick trot steps, using the voice command will initiate the same response after a few tries. By using only the voice command, I don't have to move, making it much easier for the horse to arrange his body to strike into a balanced canter. Even the movement to assume the position for the canter departure will affect their balance. I do not allow them to run into the canter if they try to because this will cause them to be out of balance from the first stride, producing anxiety. When the horse steps into a balanced canter, he will not be strong enough to carry it far before he falls on the forehand losing his balance, bracing his body and trying to speed up, so I ask for only a few strides before a downward transition. As the horse builds strength, I will ask for more steps. I am not interested in producing an unbalanced canter. I would rather have three steps of balanced canter than 30 steps of unbalanced. Endlessly cantering the horse around out of balance will not develop a good quality canter. As the horse becomes comfortable with the canter departures, I will use the voice command as I assume the canter depart aid, and eventually progress to the canter aid alone.

It's important to differentiate between the gallop and the canter. While both are three beat, they are not the same gait. Racehorses gallop, they don't canter. The gallop is momentum based and on the forehand. The canter is supposed to be generated from the hind end with the horse in self-carriage. Most ex-racers are reluctant to pick up the canter when asked in a small area such as a riding arena. This is because they only know how to gallop and it is impossible to gallop in such a small area. Retired racehorses usually develop anxiety when they realize what you are asking since they believe you want to gallop. As noted earlier, racehorses do have a slow gallop—the hobby horse—which is about the speed of a canter. Most racehorses are tense at this speed and move very rigidly. They also usually lay on the bit quite a lot.

Never run the horse into the canter. This puts the horse out of balance from the start and he has no choice but to speed up and lean on the bit to try to stay upright. If the horse speeds up when you ask, slow him, get a balanced trot and then ask again. He must step into the canter, and this takes both coordination and physical development. Remember, he's been running into the gallop for the last however many years.

Another challenge for the newly retired racehorse is picking up a specific lead. In most cases, when the horse begins his gallop on the racetrack, the rider does not ask him to pick up a lead. The horse starts jogging and at a certain point he and the rider relax together into the gallop on whichever lead the horse prefers. When they come to the place on the track where he is supposed to change, the rider asks by stepping into the stirrup of the desired lead.

When you begin asking the horse to canter, he will most likely pick up whichever lead he picked up at the start of his galloping at the track. Reward him because in his mind he has done as asked – picked up the canter. It will take him some time to realize you not only want him to canter, but you want him to pick up a particular lead. With some time, the horse will figure this out.

There are some things you can do to help the horse pick up the lead you want. For one thing, on the track, the horse gallops on the left lead around the turn and he changes to the right lead at the head of each stretch. This means, he's on a curve for the left lead and a straightaway for the right. Asking for the right lead on a circle is going to make it harder. Ask for the right lead as you come out of the turn. In addition, if you move your weight over the outside shoulder, it will make it easier for the horse to pick up the inside lead or the lead you are likely asking for. Horses are practical so if you make it easier to pick up one lead over the other, he will likely oblige you. If the horse has a preferred lead, which most do, he may not be able to maintain the canter in balance for long. Five strides can become eight strides and eight strides can become a 20-meter circle over time. It's better to canter only as far as the horse can maintain balance.

When giving the aid for the canter, don't try too hard. I see people hump, push, pull and kick the horse trying to get the correct lead. This just creates anxiety in the horse during the transition. It's already hard enough for him; don't make it even harder by throwing your body around. Simply ask for the canter depart with the correct aid for the lead you want. If you do not get it, rebalance the horse and ask again. Timing of the aid is imperative. If you ask at the correct time the horse will not have to think about it, he will react to the aid by stepping into the canter. Don't drill the horse, he needs time so just be patient.

When I begin canter work astride, here at Leighton Farm, I begin on whatever lead the horse is most resistant to picking up – usually the right. I always start with a circle, in this case to the right. Since I'm going to the right, I ask as I come out of the circle onto the long side of the arena. Initially, I sit lightly and use the voice command, "Scout….And….Canter." I don't move. It usually takes about a week for the horse to consistently pick up the canter from the voice commands alone – if I've done my homework in the canter on the lunge. Once the horse is reliably picking up the canter with voice commands, I begin pairing the physical aid with the voice command. I post the trot and put my weight into the right stirrup without leaning. I basically step into it, but not abruptly. Once my weight is where I want it, I lightly sit the trot and allow my right seat bone to move forward and to lighten. I sit to the outside without leaning but I don't take the weight out of my right stirrup. When done correctly, your right leg will be slightly ahead of your left or in other words, your outside leg will be back. Be careful not to put your outside leg too far back because this will cause you to fall to the inside. I use the voice command as I assume the canter aid position. Be clear and consistent in the application of your canter aid and then be patient. Eventually, it's easy to transition to the physical canter depart aid alone.

Occasionally I get a horse that is committed to one lead or the other. When this happens, I first confirm that it is not a lameness/soreness issue. Most of the time it's a weakness issue instead. At the track he may have been allowed to go around on the lead he preferred most of the time, developing more strength to one side. In these cases, I only ask for the lead they resist for several days to a week. I do not get upset when they pick up the wrong lead. I just ask for the trot and try again. Often, the horse is heavy on the inside shoulder so when I step into the inside stirrup while keeping my weight over the outside shoulder, I also lift my inside rein. I do not pull back, I lift.

It's best to canter only a few strides and then ask for the trot before the horse loses his balance and speeds up. Gradually extend the amount of time you canter as the horse develops. Keep in mind when a horse speeds up during the canter, he is not trying to run off, he's most likely trying to regain his balance.

When it comes time to work on flying changes, your racehorse already knows how to do them. It was an important part of his job. Changing your weight to the new stirrup is all it will take, but again, he was doing it at the gallop with the help of momentum. The next time a race is on television, watch how the jockeys get the new lead. You will never see them hike their outer leg back to get it. For the record, I do not recommend working on flying changes until the horse is physically developed enough to be off his forehand. I want my horses to have three solid, balanced gaits before I even approach the changes.

Galloping

Galloping racehorses is a specialized skill that takes years to develop as a rider, just like Eventing, Dressage and Show Jumping are highly specialized styles of riding. Lots of people get a retired racehorse and dream of galloping across the fields, the wind blowing through their hair. Such a romantic idea. The reality is, if you blast across that field not knowing how to properly gallop your horse there will be consequences and some of them may be severe. There is a position and amount of strength you must have to stay with the horse in the center of his motion. This enables the horse to balance and the rider to apply the aids effectively. Not having the skills and the strength needed can result in your horse being injured, or at the very least your horse will know you do not know what you are doing. Think about that statement for a moment. A retired racehorse doesn't know how to do dressage, a 20-meter circle or how to properly jump, but he does know how to gallop. He's been doing it for years under different riders, some of them good, some of them great, some of them not so great, but they were all professionals and they galloped horses for a living.

Your horse may not know that you are not that great at dressage because he has no experience with it, but he does know whether you know how to gallop. Racehorses learn to size up riders rather quickly since they have had many riders throughout their careers. It's survival for them to know who is in the irons. The horse can lose trust and confidence in you during a time when you are trying to build a relationship with him. This is a partnership with you as his leader in this uncharted territory called pleasure or show riding. To follow your lead, the horse needs to be able to trust that you know the way.

I strongly advise against galloping until a good dressage or flatting foundation is instilled in the retired racer. I believe it is important to send a clear message to the newly retired racehorse that he is now beginning a new chapter in his life as something other than a racehorse. Since every other discipline I know of requires the horse to come off the forehand, if you spend time galloping before you have established a topline, you will be reinforcing a frame that puts your horse on the forehand. I don't gallop horses here until they have a very solid foundation for self-carriage, which normally takes at minimum a year to develop. If I were to intersperse gallops in my training, I would be reinforcing carriage on the forehand at a time when I am trying to develop a completely new way of going for the horse. This is not only confusing for the horse, it creates a setback each time we do it. The gallop is the one thing I don't have to develop in the retired racer. It will be there when I need it.

If your goal is to eventually event your horse, then the gallop will be a part of the equation. This is the one thing you don't need to teach your horse, but you will need to learn how to gallop properly if you do not already know how. There is easy access to coaches for dressage, flat, show jumping, and cross country jumping, but little in the way of instruction on how to properly gallop. I have met people rather far up in the eventing world who did not know how to properly gallop horses. They were worried they didn't have enough "control" cross country, especially once the fences began to get bigger. If their horse wasn't an off-track Thoroughbred, he didn't know how to gallop either, since a rider without that knowledge had been his trainer.

So, how do you learn to gallop? In racing we learn to gallop on babies and as they develop, our skills and strength develop along with theirs. The "green" exercise rider also rides older "easy" horses who know how to gallop and are patient enough to allow them to make mistakes and learn from them – just like school horses in other disciplines. The other, more experienced riders teach them the ins and outs, too. You rarely gallop racehorses alone so there are always people to lend a hand and give advice.

Nowadays, with liability being such an issue, it's not so easy to find someone willing to take on a novice who aspires to learn to gallop—even when they have an eye on a professional career at the track. Many exercise riders learn on training farms before going to the racetrack. Some come from the eventing world. My best advice is to try to find an eventing trainer who is willing to give you some galloping lessons, preferably on an older, easy horse to gallop. Or if you are lucky, you might find a racehorse farm that is willing to teach you to gallop. You may even make a couple bucks once you settle in, if you are already a good rider.

Once you begin to work on galloping your horse, there are some things it will be helpful to know. For one, each horse has his own speed. By this I mean there is a speed of galloping that is easiest for that particular horse. He can relax; the rider does not need to hold him or send him. The rider merely stays in balance with the motion. When you hold/slow a horse, he hits the ground harder. When you allow him to move freely and in balance, he is the easiest on himself. This means that slower is not necessarily easier on a horse.

If you do gallop a horse with any regularity, he will get galloping fit and high spirited. He'll begin to act like a jerk in most cases and it will be your doing that caused it, not his. The only way to relieve the energy built up by the fitness developed by galloping is to breeze the horse and with more time, he will become even fitter. Eventually, he will need a race and you will be on the wrong path with your new OTTB.

The average galloping speed of most horses at the track is right around Training level speed in eventing. This means that Novice and Beginner Novice speeds must be "held." If you do not know how to hold a horse, then anxiety will creep into the picture with less than desirable results. The gallop should be relaxed and then it can be slowed with subtle iterations of the rider's body. Over-bitting to achieve the same results does not work. Holding a horse with the bit is a harmful crutch.

About Jumping

There are trainers who take horses directly from the track and begin jump training immediately. I honestly don't understand why people are so excited when a horse straight off the track can get over an obstacle. Of course, a horse bred for athleticism can jump! There was a rider in a James Wofford gymnastics clinic I was riding in who had gotten a horse from the track only the week before. He was a steeplechase trainer/rider and planned to run the horse in steeplechase races. This works well because simply put, steeplechase and hurdle horses are racehorses that race over fences.

But if you want to pursue eventing, stadium jumping, foxhunting or just recreational jumping, that approach is probably going to give you less than desirable results. Each jump challenges a horse's balance. A racehorse needs the proper tools to reclaim his balance after each fence before beginning serious jump training. Starting the horse over obstacles larger than ground poles before he has developed a topline and rear end will result in the horse falling on the forehand, grabbing the bit and running to find balance. That is all the racehorse or any horse for that matter can do before he has the strength to correct his balance by using his rear end and topline.

A solid flat work foundation is critical for the horse to build confidence when he begins jump training. If he can't rebalance himself after a fence, he is sure to begin to have anxiety about jumping. I've seen lots of retired racers over-bitted at local horse shows and normally it's very clear they do not have the flat work fundamentals to be doing the work correctly. Always remember how generous Thoroughbreds are. Most of them will try to do whatever is asked, even if it is an unfair request.

I like to introduce ground poles early in the horse's training to make him aware of where his feet are and as an excellent precursor to jumping. Ground rails provide a small, surmountable challenge to a horse's balance and highlight the need for straightness, rhythm and the rider staying with the horse—all of the requirements for jumping but at an introductory level. When you first ask a horse to step over a ground pole or jump he only knows you are pointing him at a solid object and there are two obvious ways around it. In his mind, you are asking him to take the hardest possible route for no obvious reason. You must stress straightness on approach, while stepping over and departing each ground rail. You will find that horses want to lean in one direction or another when stepping over the obstacles. Your job is to show him the way by keeping a constant rhythm and stressing the straightness to maintain balance. You do this by riding him from the leg to the hand. Imagine keeping the horse in the "tunnel" of your legs and hands. Ground rails can be tackled at the walk, trot and then canter as the horse develops. If working over poles elicits excitement from your horse, you need to address the cause before moving on to formal jump training. Trot poles can be set into countless arrangements as gymnastic exercises.

There's nothing wrong with popping over small logs here and there around the farm in the early stages. Even better, you can have another more experienced horse leading the way. This is a relaxing way to introduce the concept of jumping to the horse.

The formal introduction to jumping in the ring should be kept low key. The horse should be relaxed and in front of the leg. Don't make it a big deal. If you are tense or excited, he will sense that and mirror it.

I like to keep the duration of the initial jump sessions short. I do not want the horse to think it's a big deal. If the horse becomes excited or frightened at any stage in this training, I back up to the point where he can again be comfortable and calm, enabling him to regain confidence.

I jump twice per week. If I have to kick or cajole the horse over the jump, I'm asking too much. I want him to think it's easy and choose to do it. I gradually work the height up to about 2' at center, but this is determined by the horse, not by me. I stay at this height as we progress to multiple jumps and finally lines.

Once the horse is comfortable at the introductory stage, I begin to focus on very simple gymnastics. Gymnastics teach the horse how to jump correctly while the rider's job is to be an intelligent passenger. The gymnastic set up will teach the lesson to the horse. I believe in James Wofford's gymnastics approach to jump training. You do not have to be an eventer to use this method as it delivers a solid foundation for jumping to the horse. His book, "Gymnastics: Systematic Training for Jumping Horses" is available online and at bookstores. It has clear instructions and diagrams on how to set up gymnastics to develop proper jumping skills for the horse. The exercises start with very basic, easy to follow instructions and advance to more complicated and difficult exercises to address specific issues a horse may have. I like to pepper in simple jumping over logs and small cross-country fences between the lessons in the ring.

Keep the fences low for a long time, until the horse is "trained," meaning in front of the leg and willing to try new obstacles and rideable to and between the fences. Use this time to build confidence in the horse and to introduce all the basic questions – vertical, oxer, flowers underneath and then of course related distances. Whenever you introduce a new question, lower the fence from the horse's comfortable level of height because you are challenging him with a new concept. This applies to advanced as well as green horses. When any horse refuses a fence, obstacle, or question, you must have a plan and protocols to address it. I do not believe in hitting the horse for stopping when he is learning, so if he refuses at this point in the training, I try to figure out why and try again. When he does go, I lavish him with praise. It is most important to be fair to the horse if you are going to have a good and trusted partnership. When I do correct a horse, I must feel confident I know why the horse stopped and why I am punishing him. I only have a few seconds to make this determination and if I am unsure, I let it go. I never want to hit a horse because he was confused, in pain or didn't understand the question.

Know that when you turn away from the fence, you are re-presenting it and the horse has essentially been allowed to refuse it. As long as the horse is facing the fence, the refusal isn't consummated. If it's low enough you can ask him to step over it. If it's too high, you will need to re-present it. You can stuff a horse over a low fence, but you need the momentum of pace to get over a larger fence, so for safety's sake, you must re-present the bigger fences.

Horses don't use time to define an event. It doesn't really matter how long a horse stands before he executes a command because his brain doesn't analyze, instead it reacts. So, for the horse, his perception of the exercise will be more like "I went, I didn't, it was a good experience or a bad one." Make it a good one, no matter how long it takes. Where a water obstacle is concerned you can stand there all day until he goes, but it helps significantly if you present with a horse that loves water as a lead. If it is a 3' cross country jump before the water, then you wouldn't be able to stuff the horse over it. In that case you have had a lapse in judgment (you over faced the horse in some way) or the horse is being sticky or naughty (in which case you must correct him for refusing and then re-present.)

Shipping Off the Farm

It is important to make shipping routine for the horse. I do this by taking short trips to a friend's farm with another horse who is a confident shipper. Wherever you take your horse on these initial trips your destination should have a quiet, relaxed environment. I take the ex-racer off the trailer, graze him with the other horse, and put him in a stall while I ride the other horse. In effect, the other horse is serving as the ex-racer's pony.

I keep the first off-site experiences short, pleasant, and most important, safe. Although the horse may be accustomed to shipping, it's their first trip under my care. This initial experience sets a precedent; the horse will gauge its safety during travel with me based on this. Therefore, it's essential to make their first experience positive. Upon returning home, the horse should feel relaxed, viewing the trip as a routine task. That's why my initial trips are primarily aimed at acclimating the horse to shipping with me and ensuring they associate it with positive experiences.

The horse's mindset during the second trip will be heavily influenced by the experience of the first. Despite meticulous planning, unforeseen circumstances can occur, possibly leading to a negative experience. The subsequent trip would then be overshadowed by this unfavorable encounter, necessitating damage control by stepping back and making the trip even easier. Ignoring your horse's feelings towards travel can lead to a downward spiral, creating a horse that dislikes travel and competition. Remember, a horse's perception is directly based on past experiences. The horse's wellbeing is always the priority. Gradual trust-building is key.

Once the horse is comfortable with short trips, I ship him to a show he is not entered in or go to a park where he can be ridden with his pony buddy or a calm companion. This is a very relaxing and productive way to introduce him to this new purpose for traveling. That's the real goal here, to create circumstances where shipping is relaxing. This may take some time for some horses, but if you do it, you will never regret it. Allow it to take as long as each horse needs.

When we arrive at the new place, the horse will need to know why he is there. I do the walk/halts immediately until he focuses on me. This may take some time. But once I gain his attention, he will not be distracted by the activities and more important he will understand what to do. No matter the location or activity, the horse must focus on the handler or rider at all times.

When I have the horse entered in a clinic or show or have another planned activity, I arrive early and give the horse a chance to settle in. Most horses do well with a hand walk around the place to see it and adjust to the new environment. Some horses do well with a quiet hack around.

Lunging may help if you've trained him to do it ahead of time. Again, the horse must focus on you and obediently carry out your commands for lunging. Racing around on the lunge line without direction from you will ramp him up and excite him; not calm him down. Always remember how taxing lunging is physically and mentally for the horse and don't use it to tire him and then expect to ride in a clinic for two hours.

There's a competition arena near Leighton Farm which hosts numerous jumper shows, making it an ideal location for initial exposure to competition. I always arrive early, preferably with another horse that's already comfortable with the venue. I give my horse time to acclimate to the environment before unloading him from the trailer. A leisurely walk around the grounds, with stops for grazing, helps the horse get accustomed to the surroundings.

It's natural for the horse to be excited or on high alert at first, but most start to relax with some time. Only when the horse appears comfortable do I proceed with tacking up. This may trigger another wave of anxiety. When this happens, I calmly ride the horse around until it eases. Every horse is unique and requires different amounts of time to relax. If the horse seems overly anxious after a reasonable period, I revert to walking and grazing until he calms down. The day ends with a return home.

My ultimate goal is to cultivate a reliable competitor. Sometimes, it takes several visits to achieve the desired mental state for successful competition. As long as I prevent any negative experiences, the horse will return in a better mindset each time. Having been there and returned home safely once, the horse has a positive experience to rely on.

One thing to avoid is entering the competition arena before the horse is ready. Forcing an anxious or uncertain horse into the arena will associate the space with unease and nervousness. I can't count the number of times I've watched a disastrous warm up followed by an even more disastrous round. I can't understand why the trainer thought it was going to get any better by going into the competition arena. The horse had already told them everything they needed to know in the warmup. As I watched them head to the competition arena, I thought to myself, "Don't do it." If instead they listened to the horse and addressed whatever issues he was having, they may not have had a good show that day, but they wouldn't have made things even worse. Taking the pressure off and allowing the horse to become more comfortable with its surroundings and what is being asked of it will eventually lead to success. It's a given that horses adapt to intimidating situations when they aren't harmed, so patience is key.

If I have a horse I think will be nervous going off site to his first show, I plan short trips to my friend's farm to ride him for the five to seven days preceding the show. I took one of my more high-strung horses there to ride Monday through Friday the week before the show. The horse was on high alert the first day, but the day was easy so when we loaded up the next day to go, he was visibly more confident. By Friday, it was old hat to him. Shipping wasn't exciting anymore. Saturday was the event and he expected to get on the trailer so he was very relaxed. We shipped to the show with plenty of time to familiarize with the grounds and he left with a blue and a red in his first dressage show. I like to start the horses I train at dressage shows because they have ride times and usually are quiet. The work is also simple because the Training Level Tests are comprised of straight lines, circles and a few transitions. Once the horse has some confidence, I transition to jumper shows or whatever I feel they are suited to. My entire goal is to ensure the horse has a positive introduction to showing.

With relaxed types, I still normally begin with dressage shows, but I don't need to ship them off every day before. I will have gotten them off the farm a time or two to make sure I know how they will react. Sometimes there's an unforeseen problem lurking and you won't see it until you present the trailer. Although the more relaxed types are easier to get to showing, I do need to listen to them and address their concerns. Another horse I trained was extremely quiet. I took him off site a few times and he was easygoing about those easy trips. I then took him to his first dressage schooling show, with another horse for company. He was essentially the same as always at the trailer. When we headed down to the warmup, he stopped and I could feel he didn't like the looks of a busy arena with lots of horses. I let him look, gave him a pat and a bit of time and then gently nudged him to proceed. He walked a bit further, looked some more and eventually we made it into the arena where I allowed him to stand and watch the other horses. After ten minutes or so, he became bored. I like bored. Bored is the lack of excitement. At that point, we began to walk around and eventually to trot and canter. I was still not committed to doing the class because I always have to weigh the benefits and the risks of continuing. If I stop now and leave, we will have accomplished a lot toward creating a solid competitor. If I go on and something negative happens, we will lose that and have to do damage control on our next show outing. I have to weigh the odds. If it was hard fought to get to that point, I would probably stop for the day and take my success home. In this case, it was easy to get to this point so we continued on to a first and fourth place finish. It was a good day for him.

I ship my horses off-site to collaborate with other experts. This approach offers an additional perspective on our performance and ensures a positive experience for the horse, as interacting with skilled equestrians invariably enriches their learning. I also do this to showcase well-trained retired racers to high-level professionals and others who are present.

Every trip off the farm is important. I do everything I can to ensure that the horses are familiar and comfortable with the shipping process before embarking on significant outings. If any issues arise, I back off and make whatever adjustments are necessary to ensure their confidence and comfort during travel.□

6 WHEN THINGS GO WRONG

Every horse deserves the tools to have a great life. When we take responsibility for a retired racehorse, we owe it to him to prepare him for his life after racing. When things don't go the way we dream, it's our responsibility to find the way to get the horse on the right path. I see far too many people get a horse off the track, begin to have problems, blame the horse and discard him in his greatest time of need. Whether you get them for free or buy them, you must invest the money to have them correctly retrained or you must invest your own time and resources to teach them a new discipline. An all too common approach is to cannibalize the training retired racehorses already have for instant results. This approach sets them up for failure, emotional problems and anxiety because they were not given the tools for long term success.

It took a lot of time and work to prepare your horse to race. It is going to take more than a couple months to put a proper foundation on him to perform successfully in another discipline. You will be able to use much of his existing training in your new discipline but little of the physical and mental development from racing. The horse must be completely redeveloped both physically and mentally for all of the show and pleasure disciplines. This takes time and skill. There is no substitute for proper development, even if you seemingly get away with skipping ahead because you have a generous horse who is trying to please you.

A fundamental cause of training problems is failing to understand how different the brain of the horse is. Their brain is slightly larger than a walnut, and while they are not dumb, they are not human smart either. They are horse smart. Experts debate how much complex thought horses are capable of. They do agree, though, that the horse's first inclination is to react rather than reason. Classical Horsemanship is based on this premise. Sit on your left seat bone, the horse reacts by turning left, pull on the reins and the horse will react by going faster, and so on. Humans generally go to complex thought first and therefore tend to complicate the relationship with the horse by mistakenly thinking that horses' brains work the same way. When you ask why the horse is doing something, the answer is always the same: because you, the handler, have in some way caused the horse to react that way. If you don't like the reaction, change the stimulus. When the human blames the horse because they feel the horse decided to be difficult that day, it is extremely unfair and unproductive. A horse is designed and wired to find food, reproduce, and stay alive by avoiding aggressors. He is wired to react, not reason, and when he does react, he should not be punished. His brain does not work in such a way that he "doesn't feel like" doing something. You, the trainer/rider must find the reason the horse reacted the way he did and set him up to react the way you want.

If you operate on the premise that your horse is reacting to your handling or training, you will be successful. When you hit resistance with the horse in your training, find the reason to fix the problem. The horse may be in pain or not understand the question. He may be ramped up and overreactive due to too much grain or an unstable environment. He may not be properly prepared to fulfill the request or may have been put in a defensive position by too much pressure. When unfairly challenged, horses will become defensive, they will shut down, freak out or at the very least be unwilling to accept new challenges. It is our job as their trainer and caretaker to prepare them for what we ask, and if there is a problem to locate the source and address it. Forcing the horse to succumb to our will without regard for his concerns will eventually result in the horse letting us down because he has not been prepared to do anything else.

The true measure of a trainer is revealed in times of difficulty. Patience is the most important trait a trainer needs in order to be successful. Good horse trainers have endless patience, both with themselves and with their horses. They must have excellent self-control of their emotions, as well as their bodies. They understand

and accept that when something goes wrong, it is not the horse's fault. And they listen to the horse, because he will tell them everything they need to know.

APPENDIX

Some Lunging Basics

There is the possibility your new horse already knows how to lunge, or at least thinks he does. A lot of people who break racehorses include lunging as part of their breaking regimen. However, it probably was not done in the disciplined manner I am about to outline.

Safety should always be your primary concern when lunging a horse. Always wear protective gear such as gloves, a safety vest, and a helmet. It's crucial to ensure the lunge line never wraps around any part of your body to prevent serious injuries, which can be fatal.

When changing the horse's direction, avoid letting the lunge line drag on the ground as it may entangle in the horse's legs or around you. Choose a contained area with good footing to start training. Racehorses are conditioned to accelerate from a standstill to racing speed, so they might bolt when frustrated. This sudden movement can lead to injuries, hence a round pen is ideal for initial lunge training. An indoor or small paddock are good alternatives.

Never wrap the lunge line around your hand. Fold it back and forth and hold it in the middle.

For effective lunge training, you'll need a 45-foot lunge line and a lunging cavesson or a bridle. A lunge whip is necessary; remember it serves as the leg aid not a punishment tool. Consider using protective boots or polo bandages to protect the horse's legs.

Every horse is unique, but there's a basic format for lunging. Always lunge in tack, a cavesson or bridle, and saddle, ensuring the reins are removed or twisted through the throatlatch to prevent injury. The chain on the lunge line should go through the bit, over the nose, and clipped to the other side of the bit. This is familiar to racehorses. However, if a horse shows discomfort, consider using the fabric lunge line over the nose instead.

The initial days should include behavior modification along the fence before introducing lunging in the arena. Avoid overexerting the horse; a calm, relaxed walk is the goal. Transitioning to trotting should only occur once the horse is comfortable walking and halting on the circle in both directions. Rushing into trotting or cantering can cause physical harm and anxiety.

Some horses may be tense initially, especially if they've experienced stressful lunging in the past. Starting with a walk can help them relax. The goal is for them to comfortably walk in a circle around you and respond to "Ho" by halting. Consistency is key at this stage. The horse may struggle to maintain balance in a circle, which can be frightening at first. Therefore, patient and gradual training is the best approach, starting with no more than five minutes in each direction.

The quality of the walk should not be overlooked; insist on an active, marching walk. Once you achieve a good, relaxed walk, progress to a slow, balanced trot – no rushing or uncontrolled movements. The horse should display self-carriage and relaxation. If he speeds up, transition back to a walk, then return to a trot again. Keep trotting periods short until he maintains rhythm and balance, then proceed to canter using the same method.

Steps to Lunging

Use the commands for walk and halt that you used in the behavior modification. Add "Horse name, AND Trot and Horse Name AND Canter" for consistency. It is also possible to control the horse's speed and pace with voice aids in addition to his gaits. I use the word "easy" spoken in a soothing way with a gentle tug of the line to get him to slow. If the horse doesn't respond I growl and give him another tug sometimes saying "Hey! Hey! Hey!". Commands such as "walk on," "trot on," "canter," "Ho" and "easy" are also universally employed by trainers. Use intonation to help with upward and downward transitions. Let your voice go from low to high for upward transitions such as halt to walk, walk to trot and trot to canter transitions. Let your voice go from high to low for canter to trot, trot to walk and walk to halt transitions. The walk to halt command should sound final. Show the horse the whip for upward transitions and point it down and away from the horse for downward transitions.

Put the chain over the horse's nose as you did in the behavior modification. Once the horse is confirmed at or has accepted lunging you can take the chain off the lunge line and just put the cloth lunge line over the nose. In the past I advocated putting the lunge line through the bit, over the poll and attached to the other side of the bit as pictured below, but I now know this is terrible for the horse. The lunge line acts like a vice by creating immense pressure on the poll while at the same time pulling the bit hard up into the mouth. Please do not ever use this method while lunging your horse.

Position yourself in the center of the ring. This is your "home" position. If you're lunging to the left, hold the lunge line in your left hand and the whip in your right hand. Fold the lunge line back and forward over itself in your hand. Make sure it's not twisted and feels comfortable in your hand. Never wrap it around your hand. Stand in your home position facing the middle of the horse's body, forming one point of an imaginary triangle, the lunge line hand to the horses mouth forming another point and the whip to the horse's butt forming the other point.

Stay in the home position as much as possible. Pivot on one foot as the horse moves around the circle to help keep yourself from meandering. Staying in one place helps to keep the horse relaxed. It also requires the horse to do a true circle rather than various iterations of ovals. Accurate circles make the horse work his inside hind leg effectively. Send the horse out on the circle by asking for walk and letting the lunge line slip through your fingers. Do not allow him to run out, insist he walk. In the beginning the horse will not do a perfect circle. He will cut in. Do not make a big deal of this for the first day or two, just keep the lunge line out of his way, by shortening and letting it back out. Be careful not to let it wrap around your hand or feet. In the following days you will encourage the horse to stay out on a perfect circle by pointing the whip at his head or shoulder. Remember, you want a big circle. Point the whip slightly behind the horse to ask him to go and point it behind you when not giving a signal. Be relaxed and calm in your body and voice.

If the horse halts and gets stuck. try not to go out to him and to fix it unless necessary. When you do this, you are giving the horse control. He stops, you come out to him. If you must get after him, step out of your "home position" toward him, flopping the whip and the voice command "Go on", but as soon as he moves off, go back to the home position and continue. If you can't get him to make the decision to move off, then go out and restart him.

To halt the horse, say "Ho" in a final way and lower your voice, if he doesn't stop, say it again more firmly. When teaching the horse to stop you can head him into the wall or fence as you say "Ho." Keep the horse from turning in or falling in on the circle by pointing the whip at the horse's head. He should be far enough away from you that there is no chance the whip could come in contact with him. Do not reel the horse in to you; this teaches the horse to run at you, or even over you.

To lunge the horse in the other direction first halt the horse and when he has stopped, walk out to him, do not reel him in to you, taking in the lunge line as you go. Make sure you fold the lunge line rather than roll it, to lessen the danger of it tightening around your hand if the horse takes off. Change the lunge line to the opposite side of the bit, and then walk back to the center of the circle as you encourage him to walk out on in the new direction. I have found this helps the horse understand you are not leading him, you are lunging him. Do not put the whip on the ground while you work on the horse. People have been injured or killed by bending down to pick up the whip off the ground.

If the horse tends to jackknife, I will put a very loose side rein on the outside only. Under normal circumstances, when the horse is comfortable lunging both ways, I put on both side reins very loosely, because the correct use of side reins is for the horse to reach to them—not for them to hold the horse's head down or restrict him in any way. The horse should reach to and follow the contact with the rider's hands. They should be a comfortable place for the horse to share contact. Used properly, side reins introduce the trusted contact and educated mouth we wish to carefully develop on the horse. The side reins coupled with the circle are a very effective way to start building both muscle and the skills needed in a riding horse.

If you decide to employ trotting poles while lunging, begin with one. When the horse is comfortable with it, go to two. Do not rush this process. Trotting poles make the horse look where he's putting his feet, which is a fundamental of jump training. This stretches his topline.

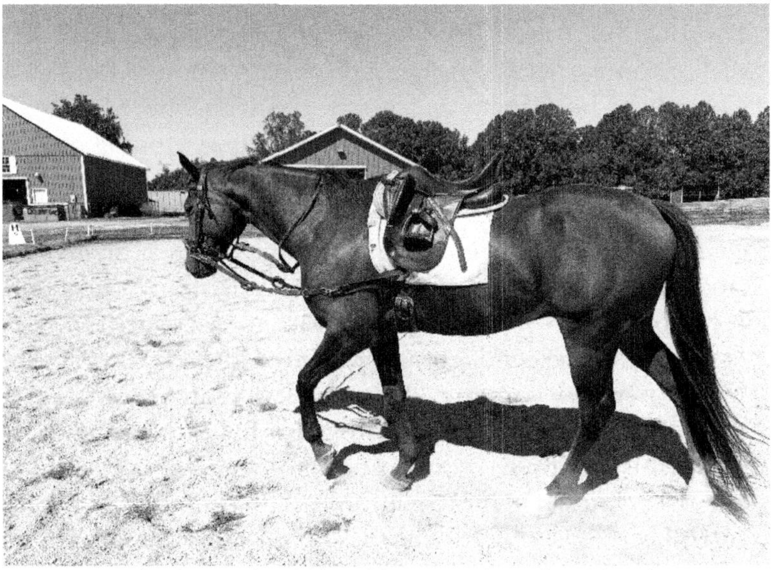

The horse should be able to reach to the side reins.

ABOUT THOROUGHBRED PLACEMENT RESOURCES, INC.

OUR MISSION

Thoroughbred Placement Resources, Inc. improves the lives of Thoroughbred racehorses, both active and retired by providing training and rehabilitation while educating the public through the development of Breed Ambassadors.

We Create breed ambassadors

Not long ago the Thoroughbred was the breed of choice for American riders. Thoroughbreds such as Bally Cor, Jet Run, and Touch of Class enjoyed great success in the Olympic equestrian disciplines, but today many riders favor other breeds. With proper training and exposure, Thoroughbreds can be at the top of the show world again. Success with these horses will have a trickle-down effect. Owners and adopters will seek trainers who have experience with retired Thoroughbred racehorses and this will increase their value. There will be more success stories and fewer failures. Linda Zang states, "There have been many success stories with Thoroughbreds in the three Olympic Equestrian disciplines, including winning medals. "

Presenting properly trained Thoroughbreds to top trainers is an important element of what we do. The more other riders and trainers hear icons such as George Morris, Joe Fargis, Ann Kursinski, and Linda Zang extol the virtues of Thoroughbreds, the more demand and appreciation there will be for retired racehorses. The horses have to be present at clinics and competitions or they can't talk about them. That's where we come in. We bring the examples of correctly trained retired racers and present them. Turn the tide and ultimately, we will see Thoroughbreds competing and winning at the highest levels, in all disciplines. Then many more will find homes after racing.

Currently, keeping a retired Thoroughbred racehorse and putting the correct training on him costs more than the seller can recoup. The same amount of training on a Warmblood will pay about twice what a comparable Thoroughbred will bring. This causes people to get horses off the track and move them on quickly for a few thousand dollars where they will likely be resold again. This does not provide the training the horse needs to be desirable to upper level trainers. We can address this by selecting excellent Thoroughbred candidates and giving them the proper training they need. This will make them attractive to top riders. This will increase their value substantially.

We Provide help for horses with Training issues

Today retired racers are regaining their popularity as riding horses. Racetracks are creating programs to help find them homes once their race careers end. Moving horses off of the track quickly has become less of a crisis. There are consequences though. When moving a great number of horses into the hands of the public, more than a few end up with people who are not qualified to handle and retrain a horse directly off the track. In Dr. Andrew Mclean's book, "The Truth About Horses" he references a study by researchers Odberg and Bouisseau. They found that of 3,000 non-racing horses sent to the slaughterhouse in France between the ages of two and seven years, 66.4% were condemned for "inappropriate behavior." The fact that these statistics come from countries with well-established equestrian traditions gives no grounds for believing that the figures would be much different elsewhere.

We Provide help for Horses in need of Surgery or Rest and Rehabilitation

In addition to Thoroughbreds with training issues, there are horses who leave racing with physical problems. These can be successfully addressed through surgery or rest and rehabilitation. Horses like these are difficult to place due to the cost of rehabilitation and the skills needed to correctly rest and rehabilitate them. In many cases, proper rest and rehab results in an excellent prognosis and a sound horse ready for a qualified adoption.

TPR has these specialized skills to address these high-risk categories of horses. Leighton Farm, the home base of TPR was designed for active racehorses to rest and rehabilitate. In addition, Kimberly Godwin Clark, principal equestrian at Leighton Farm was a professional exercise rider, owner and trainer with over 25 years. During these years working at the track as a rider, trainer and racehorse owner, Godwin Clark took many horses to the farm for rest and rehabilitation giving her a quarter century of experience in properly handling horses. She now works with some of the top show trainers in the United States in order to develop her skills to produce correctly retrained and rideable retired racehorses.

We educate those who have or wish to have a retired racer.

Kimberly Godwin Clark, the founder of TPR has written this book to promote correct training methods. Offering insight into the life the horse had as a racehorse providing a better understanding of ex-racers. In 2016 it was published on Kindle and Amazon in both print and electronic formats and then revised and updated in 2024. Clark is currently working on a second book that focuses on training horses and addressing problems that occur during the training process.

Additionally, Godwin Clark launched a blog that focuses on understanding and retraining these wonderful horses.

We work directly with volunteers to help them develop the skills to work with retired racehorses.

Kimberly Godwin Clark and Flatfoot Scotty.

Kimberly Godwin Clark, executive director of Thoroughbred Placement Resources, has devoted her life to the Thoroughbred breed. Clark galloped, trained and owned Thoroughbred racehorses for over 25 years, and has spent the last decade transitioning them to new disciplines once their racing careers end. This experience has given her unique insight into transitioning and retraining this wonderful breed for new equestrian disciplines.

Printed in Great Britain
by Amazon

59551272R00088